Cybersecurity for NGOs

Attack Prevention and Threat Response

Stéphane Duguin
CEO of Protect.ngo

WILEY

Published by John Wiley & Sons, Inc., Hoboken, New Jersey.

Library of Congress Control Number: 2026943220

ISBN: 9781394401239 (Paperback)
ISBN: 9781394401253 (ePDF)
ISBN: 9781394401246 (ePub)

Cover Design: Wiley
Cover Image: Cloudyew/stock.adobe.com
SKY10162199_071026

Contents

Preface

In recent years, nonprofit organizations have become lifelines for communities in need—offering food to the hungry, shelter to the displaced, education to the underserved, and hope to the vulnerable. Now these same organizations face a grave new threat: cyberattacks. When I began partnering with nonprofits through Microsoft's social impact programs, I was struck by their selflessness and vital missions. I also saw cyber threats jeopardizing their work. It became clear that protecting nonprofits in cyberspace is not just a technical concern—it is a humanitarian imperative.

Nonprofits today operate amid a cyber threat landscape that continues to intensify. In the last four years alone, Protect.ngo identified 155,993 cyberattacks against nonprofits. Email-based threats targeting the sector have risen by 35.2%, and credential phishing has surged by 50.4%. State-sponsored hackers from Russia, China, Iran, and North Korea increasingly set their sights on NGOs, think tanks, and human rights defenders. Academia, think tanks, and NGOs were among the most targeted sectors for nation-state attack notifications by Microsoft in 2025. This is particularly concerning because many nonprofits hold sensitive data on vulnerable populations but lack the resources for robust cybersecurity, making them prime targets.

Yet we are not powerless. Even as threats escalate, a spirit of resilience and collaboration is rising. A global community of "cyber-peacekeepers" is rallying to defend those on the front lines of humanitarian action. One inspiring example is Protect·ngo (formerly known as the CyberPeace Institute), an independent organization founded in 2019. Through its Cyber Builders program, it connects a global network of some 1,500 volunteer cybersecurity experts with nonprofits in need—providing free training and emergency cyber defense. These measures are essential—especially given that a foundational step as straightforward as enabling multi-factor authentication can stop 99% of attacks on NGOs. More than 650 organizations have already been helped, proving that solidarity and innovation can prevail against even the most determined threat actors.

At Microsoft, supporting nonprofits is a priority. Microsoft Elevate—our organization supporting schools, community colleges, and nonprofits globally—works alongside initiatives like our Security Program for Nonprofits, which provides free security assessments, training, and advanced threat notifications through AccountGuard, now operating across 32 countries with more than 1,500 threat notifications issued. We partner with nearly one million nonprofits and education systems worldwide, and in the coming year will deliver more than $5 billion in discounts, donations, and grants to help nonprofit organizations address community needs. But technology alone is not enough—partnership and collective action are key. That is why we collaborate with NGOs, governments, and industry peers to share threat intelligence, build cyber skills, and craft solutions tailored to the nonprofit context.

This book was born out of an urgent need to confront the realities behind these challenges—and to celebrate the courage of the nonprofit heroes who refuse to be intimidated. Within these pages, you will find stories of networks restored, of volunteers fortifying a charity's digital walls, and of alliances that prevented hospitals and refugee services from being brought down by hackers.

I hope this preface and the chapters that follow inspire both urgency and optimism. We stand at a turning point: cyber threats are escalating, but so are our collective efforts to counter them. Now is the moment to act. Protecting nonprofits in cyberspace is a shared responsibility—one that demands innovation, collaboration, and unwavering commitment. By coming together across sectors, we can ensure that those who serve humanity are themselves safeguarded.

Let us stand as guardians for the guardians, fortifying the digital defenses of organizations that uplift our communities. By protecting nonprofits from cyber threats, we protect the people and ideals they serve—and move closer to a just, resilient, and peaceful world for all.

—Justin Spelhaug, President, Microsoft Elevate

Introduction

When I was contacted to write this book, my first reaction was hesitation. How could I write a book about a subject as fluid and ever-changing as cybersecurity? How could technological innovation and criminal mutations—all short-term—be reconciled with the time it would take to gather testimonies, to reflect, to write, and to publish? During the writing process, changes would no doubt occur within the technological, criminal, or regulatory environments, changes which might be so deep that the book's publication might become obsolete.

While we were discussing this obstacle with our partners, another question, this one even more central, arose. It wasn't about navigating these barriers or finding a solution for how to write this book—it was about *why*. In the era of real-time communication, of the proliferation of snackable content, and of magical pocket prompts answering our every question, what would be the use of a physical object, held down by an unmoving temporality? *Why* write a book?

To answer this question, we must clarify a common misconception. The subject of our work, and of this book, isn't cybersecurity. In fact, generally, when speaking of cybersecurity, we are ultimately speaking of entirely different things. Addressing cybersecurity means addressing water sanitation, world hunger, the protection of children, humanitarian aid, climate change, and the defense of democracy. Cybersecurity is always a means, never an end; therefore, these discussions are not about volatile pieces of code evolving alongside the creativity of criminals. They are about the timeless need to secure urgent and fundamental human needs. When it comes to attacks against nonprofits, the subject is infinitely more human than it is technical.

So, when Wiley, my publisher, contacted me to suggest that I write a book, I thought, why not—a book. This project echoes my decision to lead Protect^ngo (formerly known as the CyberPeace Institute). The vision of its founders—Microsoft, the Mastercard Center for Inclusive Growth, and the William and Flora Hewlett Foundation—was to create an independent entity, a long-lasting space made of durable connections in the midst of a decimated environment. A place where the suffering of vulnerable individuals would be heard, where the energy of those defending them would be received, and where donors, politicians, cyber experts, and victims could work actively toward systemic change.

Thirty years of tracking cybercriminals and gathering testimonies from victims, notably during my years working for Europol, the law enforcement agency of the European Union, taught me one important thing: the ambition for peace and safety in cyberspace will be achieved through coalitions and connections. It will be achieved when cybersecurity technicians connect to the suffering on humanitarian frontlines. It will be reached when regulators connect to the challenges of protecting civil society organizations (CSOs). It will be reached when donors connect to the financial needs of CSOs in order to defend themselves in cyberspace. Writing this book is part of this ambition.

I see this book as a tool for all parties involved in the safety of CSOs in cyberspace. I see it as a practical object, which can serve as a glossary, a reference, food for thought, and most importantly, a call to action. I see it as a guide to be packed along at the start of a long adventure. Fittingly—since we were born in Geneva—I see it as a Swiss army knife for anyone who wishes to participate in protecting those who protect us.

How to Use This Book

This book is merely a collection of recorded actions taken to safeguard CSOs in the face of cyberattacks, particularly in the last few years as they have become increasingly frequent and aggressive. Some of these defensive actions were met with success; others were not. This path toward resilience—made of trial, error, and solidarity—belongs to a community that comes together each day for the public good. In this spirit, I would like to warmly thank all the people who offered their contribution to this book: CSO leaders and staff, cybersecurity experts, foundations, cyber volunteers, and others. You will find their testimonies and valuable insight throughout the book.

See this object as you wish: an instruction manual, a strategic guide, an informational compendium, or a testimony repository. Read it from end to end or pick and choose the information that interests you or is relevant to your situation. Whether you are part of a nonprofit as an employee, a leader, or a volunteer; have the power to enact rules and regulations; or have the ability to use your voice to make a difference, I am convinced that you will get something useful out of it. But most importantly, at the end of the day, I want you to see this book for what it is: an invitation to join our cause.

You will find information sheets filled with practical advice, some of it very easily applied, in the sections named "Actions for Resilience" at the end of Chapter 2 and "Actions for Accountability" at the end of Chapter 3.

Are you a nonprofit? Put in place simple control tools, train your staff, and raise awareness among your donors and collaborators. We are at your disposal, as well as other organizations, to offer effective, free, and targeted support.

Do you represent a state or work alongside decision-makers? You have the power to put rules into place and make sure they are respected. If your voice carries, speak out. There can never be enough testimony to the human suffering caused by cyberattacks.

Are you a philanthropy? You have the means to support organizations as they put efficient tools and processes in place for their protection. Make sure you provide nonrestrictive funding, that you support the organizational development of nonprofits, and that you encourage other donors or foundations to watch over their beneficiaries' cybersecurity. Nonprofits have a dire need for resources to defend themselves.

The options are numerous, but whatever you do, I ask you to please take these pages as a call to action. There is urgency. And if, for you, that means closing this book now and never reading it to the end, I won't be offended, so long as you join in the collective effort to face this crisis.

Become a volunteer:

`https://protect.ngo/the-builders`

https://www.cybervolunteers.us/en

Partner with us:

https://www.protect.ngo/act-now

A Note on Methodology

In this book, I'll introduce many real-life examples of attacks that have been led against CSOs and other individuals or organizations dedicated to defending human rights. These victims will not be named, and I will avoid revealing any details that would help identify them. My objective with these examples is to show you the very real threats looming in cyberspace and the way these threats operate, so that you may prepare and protect yourself as best you can. This isn't about pointing fingers or about further enhancing the vulnerability of these organizations.

Likewise, I won't name any specific attackers—they are not the subject of this book. I'm not here for sensationalism or to advertise for cybercriminals. But we will go through several standard profiles and the motivations behind the attacks led by each, specifically in Chapter 3, because understanding the threats can only lead to better protection for the victims.

You will find a more detailed section on methodology at the end of the book, along with a glossary of cybersecurity terms.

PERSPECTIVE: Protect.ngo Executive Board

In my day job, I run a federation of water and sanitation organizations working in some of the most challenging environments in the world. Staff in remote locations, sensitive data on vulnerable communities, partner organizations with limited resources. Cybersecurity is not the first thing on anyone's mind. The mission is.

And that's exactly the problem. Because when an NGO gets breached, it's not just data that's exposed. It can be the identities of human rights defenders. The locations of field staff. The trust of communities who shared sensitive information because they believed it would be protected. The consequences aren't abstract. They're personal.

What I've learned as Chair of Protect.ngo is that the sector isn't ignoring cybersecurity out of negligence. It's that the threat feels distant and technical, while the human crisis in front of you feels immediate and real. The challenge is helping organizations see that protecting their digital infrastructure is protecting their mission, not a distraction from it.

Protect·ngo exists to close that gap, with practical support that meets NGOs where they are, not where a cybersecurity vendor wishes they were. This book is part of that work. If you lead or work in a CSO, it's for you.

—Andrew McCracken, Chair of the Executive Board, Protect·ngo; Global Director, WaterAid International

PERSPECTIVE: Protect·ngo Staff

Traditional critical-infrastructure doctrine was built to protect the largest number of people from the most visible physical threats, yet in the cyber age some of the deepest harms fall on the most vulnerable populations.

Across decades working in cybersecurity in the private sector, government, international organizations, and the humanitarian world, we repeatedly encountered the same reality: organizations protecting the most vulnerable often have the least capacity to protect them, and themselves, in the digital space.

The imbalance is structural. Cybersecurity expertise is scarce and therefore expensive, while mission-driven organizations rarely have the resources to build dedicated technical teams. At the same time, thousands of cybersecurity professionals across the private sector want to use their skills for the public good, yet too often there is no clear, trusted, and structured way for them to do so.

As cofounders of the Builders [Protect·ngo's cybervolunteering program; see Chapter 4 for more information], we didn't just want to name a gap—we wanted to build a bridge. We worked hard to design and test a model capable of

(*continued*)

(*continued*)

turning goodwill and expertise into practical, reliable, and scalable support for CSOs. Not to replace the responsibility of states, but to provide a concrete response while broader systemic solutions take shape.

Collaboration is at the core of the initiative, and it's through collaboration that the Builders have helped countless mission-driven organizations respond to thousands of incidents, patch vulnerabilities, prevent data leaks, and strengthen their ability to protect the people they serve.

Helping steward that collective effort remains both a privilege and a responsibility.

—Adrien Ogée, Chief Operations Officer
Fabien Leimgruber, Head of Cyber Resilience
Alexandru Lazar, Nonprofit Cyber Resilience Specialist
Cofounders of the Builders, Protect.ngo

CHAPTER

1

Who Is Under Attack and Why?

One of the things that stand out the most from my time living in the Netherlands is cycling. For a French person, it's a series of small wonders. The cycling infrastructure: clean and flawless. Car drivers: polite and considerate. The rain, tenacious and horizontal, always finds a way through your clothes.

On 30 September 2024, as I pedal under torrential rain, exiting the forest of Scheveningen, I am filled with awe. The Peace Palace stands, a castle from another time, a majestic lighthouse in the heart of the city. For 125 years, the Palace has harbored the most ambitious peace and justice initiatives. Today, it hosts a conversation about a different frontline—one that rarely appears in peace treaties or security doctrines.

Inside, the clatter of coffee mugs fades as the audience takes its place. It is a disparate crowd. The curious stares suggest that these are not people accustomed to being in the same room together. I suspect that some are here out of habit, or by default, without particular expectation. I do not blame them. Too often, cybersecurity conferences follow a familiar script: grim observations, shared concern, and, after hours of lamentation, innovation by proclamation. We invoke the need for "better information sharing," "breaking silos," and "stronger public-private partnerships." Since 2022, many gatherings have added a final chapter of AI solutionism. Satisfied, we shake hands and book flights to the next venue.

This meeting feels different.

The speech of Tawakkol Karman, Nobel Peace Prize laureate, cuts through abstraction. A war is being waged against civil society. The Internet is its crime scene. Civil society organizations (CSOs)—those protecting refugees, delivering care, fighting climate change, purifying water, defending children, extending humanitarian aid—are not collateral damage. They are targets.

On stage, their realities unfold one after another. Women and men working at the frontlines of crises describe disruption, intrusion, exhaustion, fear. These organizations are the connective tissue of our societies in moments of breakdown. They operate where states withdraw, where markets fail, and where trust is hardest to sustain. And precisely because of this role, they are increasingly targeted—often silently, often repeatedly.

Outrage alone will not protect them. Jan van Zanen, Mayor of The Hague, home to hundreds of civil society organizations, voices the urgency. We are gathered in a place long associated with peace and justice, not to diagnose the problem once more, but to confront a reality too often ignored: civil society is being structurally exposed in cyberspace.

This moment did not emerge in isolation.

When we started our operations in Geneva in 2019, we observed a growing pattern. Across regions and sectors, CSOs were facing cyber incidents that disrupted operations, exposed beneficiaries, and strained already limited resources. From Geneva—a city shaped by humanitarian action, multilateral processes, and technical norm-setting—we focused on documenting what was happening to CSOs themselves.

Investigations accumulated. Reports were produced. Comparisons across cases revealed a consistent dynamic: while the technical characteristics of attacks varied, their consequences for organizations were systematically underestimated. Financial loss and system downtime captured only part of the damage. Lost trust, operational paralysis, staff exhaustion, and interrupted services were rarely visible, let alone addressed.

Over time, it became clear that what was missing was not concern, but understanding. Before any discussion of responsibility or remedy, a more basic task remained: recognizing what cyber threats actually do to civil society organizations—and why that matters beyond the digital domain.

The gathering at the Peace Palace marked the point at which these observations could no longer remain dispersed. It emerged as a collective acknowledgment that civil society's exposure is not incidental, but systemic—and that fragmented responses are no longer sufficient.

This book starts from there.

To understand what is at stake, we must first be clear about what civil society organizations are and the roles they play. We must also examine the context in which they now operate—a world marked by overlapping crises, widening inequalities, and growing pressures on those who provide protection where others cannot. Only then can we begin to grasp why civil society has become a frontline in cyberspace, and what it would take to ensure that those who protect the most vulnerable are not left to absorb digital risk alone.

What Are Civil Society Organizations?

To understand why CSOs have become a frontline in cyberspace, let's dive into what they are and why they matter.

The threats we are trying to address affect a wide and diverse set of actors, commonly grouped under the term "civil society organizations" (CSOs). This umbrella includes nonprofits, nongovernmental organizations (NGOs), charities, associations, and other mission-driven groups working in the public interest.

They may use a range of different terms to define themselves, depending on their structure, funding, or legal status. They are organizations committed to the public good, operating within many different sectors: health, poverty, access to drinking water, finance, energy, women's rights, hunger, education, humanitarian relief, development, human rights, climate, information, aid to migrants, peace, social services, justice. . . They are present in all regions of the world, in cities and rural areas alike, and respond to all types of emergencies. They are essential entities for the well-being and implementation of the fundamental rights of all human beings. Without CSOs, many communities would be left to their own devices when facing emergencies and difficulties arising from their circumstances, their place of residence, their government, or individuals seeking to harm them.

Across these pages, I will use the terms "nonprofit," "nongovernmental organization" (NGO), "civil society organization" (CSO), and "civil society actor" interchangeably. For the purpose of this book, while their exact definitions contain nuances, I will include all nonprofits within the scope of CSOs.

In Which Context Are They Operating Today?

We live in an era where crises no longer arrive one at a time. They converge and compound—war, political instability, information manipulation, and digital threats increasingly collide, overwhelming society's ability to respond in a highly volatile international environment. This context does not impact us in the same way, depending on where we are and the support available to us. People living in precarious conditions become more vulnerable every day. The urgency is felt when climate disasters, corruption, or poverty exacerbate the already difficult living conditions of some individuals. The gap between the most privileged and the most vulnerable is widening.

At the center of this storm sits civil society. In this geopolitical context, CSOs play a critical role. They do the work that the public sector no longer does, and that the private sector won't, acting as the connective tissue of social resilience. They play a central role in protecting the human rights of over 1 billion vulnerable individuals worldwide.

Why Is Civil Society Under Attack?

When we consider the enormous number of people all over the world who rely on the work of CSOs, it seems absurd that anyone would want to attack them. Who would act with the intention of harming them, and more importantly, why? Unfortunately, they are not random targets. Through detailed analysis, we can determine that there are systemic reasons behind this phenomenon.

Risk Profile: Who They Are and How They Operate

A CSO is an entity created in response to an event that acts as a trigger. An incident reveals a need that isn't being addressed, and the CSO defines its mission and builds itself around this goal, often very quickly in order to respond to the urgency of the situation. These structures are therefore entirely based on the goodwill of people who are determined to tackle a problem and who invest all their energy in doing so.

Due to this mode of operation, which is almost entirely focused on the nonprofit's field mission, problems often arise in relation to the implementation of nonoperational processes. In other words, issues of governance, accounting, and IT are relegated to the background as nonprofit staff and volunteers focus their time, energy, and resources on the support they bring to local individuals and communities. It can be difficult for CSOs to hire and retain staff in positions of governance or IT; often, workers are volunteers or they handle multiple roles and functions. This is precisely what creates gaps in the functioning of nonprofits, as support positions like these, often overlooked, are necessary for their longevity. Cybersecurity in particular depends on governance—decisions made in the areas of technology and data, risk appetite, and the like. In the United States, while there are 1.1 million cybersecurity professionals, half a million positions in the sector remain vacant.

The donations CSOs receive and depend on often come with restrictions and are earmarked for a specific program or project. Donors, especially those making substantial donations, want to see concrete results from their commitment and are also focused on the field mission of the CSOs that they support. This is perfectly understandable: when we care about a cause and dedicate a significant sum to it, we expect the funds to be invested directly in that mission, or in the part of that mission that is most visible.

The smooth operation of the organization may seem secondary, but in reality, it is essential to help as many people as possible.

We often say that CSOs appear to be *cyber-poor and target-rich*. *Cyber-poor*, because they may seem like easy prey, as their cybersecurity is often inadequate. Our work has shown that only one in ten nonprofits regularly trains its staff in cybersecurity; one in four monitors its networks; and one in five has a cybersecurity plan. *Target-rich*, because the sector raises more than $1 trillion a year to fund programs for communities in need, as well as holds huge amount of valuable information and data.

CSOs often operate in regions where infrastructure is limited or unreliable, and they depend on loose volunteer networks, which exposes them to threats. They may be required to work in war zones, using faulty networks, obsolete systems, and makeshift software (Figure 1.1).

These various factors make them extremely vulnerable to the full range of cyberattacks: DDoS (distributed denial-of-service), hack-and-leak, website defacement, cyberespionage, phishing campaigns, data deletion operations, and more. I will discuss the main types of attacks targeting civil society in more detail in Chapter 2.

Risk Profile: What They Do

In addition to the systemic vulnerabilities that exist in any CSO, it is sometimes the very nature of their mission that increases their exposure to risk. CSOs are on many frontlines. Inevitably, like all those who try to bring about real change in the world, through their actions and beliefs, they make enemies. This fuels the motivations of cybercriminals, states, and hacktivists, who may then take action.

Some attacks are purely motivated by a desire to hinder the organization's mission; this may be the case, for example, when it

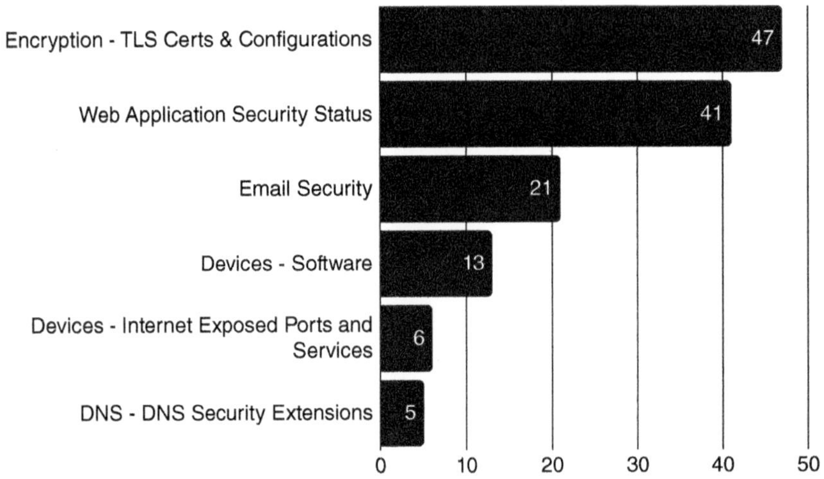

FIGURE 1.1 Breakdown of nonprofit vulnerability categories. Note: Out of 95 organizations assessed, 64 were found to have vulnerabilities. The chart shows the number of organizations affected by each category; some organizations are included in multiple categories.

Source: Protect.ngo (formerly known as the CyberPeace Institute), 2025

denounces information manipulation campaigns or provides assistance to people in certain regions of the world. In October 2025, from a Russian-owned server, a PDF file resembling a government communique was sent by email to multiple nonprofits providing assistance to the Ukrainian population, and to government administrations in Ukraine. The file contained a link to a website that required the user to check an "I am not a robot" box. This action triggered the download of malware designed to extract data from the victims' computers. It was a case of large-scale phishing. Following this attack, the common mission of the targets and the origin of the server revealed the ideological objectives of the attackers, who likely stood to gain from hindering the work of nonprofits operating in Ukraine and other Ukrainian entities.

We ourselves at Protect·ngo, as an organization that tracks and exposes cyberattacks against civil society, are not immune to these risks. Our platforms and staff are regularly targeted by attacks aimed at silencing us. We've lost track of the number of phishing emails seemingly coming from employees, human resources, or myself. Some of them, rather than being part of large phishing campaigns, target us specifically: they might contain, for example, a link to a website that looks exactly like ours, but will steal the employee's credentials if they try to sign in (this is called *spear phishing*; I will explain this type of attack in more detail in Chapter 2). Our work on Ukraine also ruffles feathers; our Cyber Attacks in Times of Conflict (CATC) platform, which tracks cyberattacks carried out in the context of the war between Ukraine and Russia, suffered the consequences of an incident that rendered the site inoperable for several minutes. This kind of attack, named DDoS (distributed denial-of-service), consists in flooding the target network with useless requests in order to put it out of service. Although the attackers did manage to render our platform inaccessible, our defense strategy was successful, and our teams were able to restore access within a few minutes.

These two examples show that the work carried out by CSOs is disruptive and increases the potential grounds for attack. Any action taken in support of a cause often provokes an opposing reaction from individuals who wish to hinder it. Their motives may be financial, political, or ideological, but in all cases, they benefit from preventing aid from reaching vulnerable communities. Often, doing good involves denouncing evil, and taking a stand also means taking a risk.

PERSPECTIVE: Protect·ngo Staff

In a polarized world, where the law of the strongest and the predator prevails, it is increasingly necessary to support those who think differently, those who help vulnerable communities. The actions of Protect·ngo (previously known as the CyberPeace Institute) therefore become even more important and necessary.

What allows us, at times, to truly make a difference is nothing other than the human relationship we have managed to build with the NGOs.

This strong bond alone has enabled us to act quickly when it was needed, and also to show that these people are not alone in their struggle to help others; this brings them reassurance.

All the technologies in the world can, of course, help us act faster and more effectively, but only human connection truly changes the game.

For the future, it is essential to strengthen this bond. Most small and medium-sized NGOs have neither the means nor the resources to take care of their cybersecurity.

Offering them services that are increasingly tailored to their needs, or even becoming part of their infrastructure, is certainly part of the solution. But to do so, we must be able to scale up, be sufficiently stable, and have enough resources so that NGOs can work with peace of mind.

—Florent Bitschy, Chief Information and Security Officer, Protect·ngo

PERSPECTIVE: Protect.ngo Staff

There is an old story about a village that was repeatedly attacked at night. At first, each household tried to protect itself. Some reinforced their doors. Others stayed awake to keep watch. A few could afford better helmets or stronger shields, while the rest hoped they would not be the next to be targeted. Everyone was doing something—yet no one truly felt safe.

One day, someone proposed a different approach. Instead of facing the threat in isolation, the villagers came together. They compared what they were seeing: where the attacks originated, which defenses held, which failed. They shared tools, coordinated their watch, and trained side by side. They did not all wear the same armor—but they learned how to defend collectively.

What changed was not only their level of protection. It was trust. The village became harder to attack not because every house was fortified, but because no one was left alone, unseen, or unsupported.

This is what protecting nonprofits means in practice. Today, CSOs face an increasing convergence of digital threats—cyberattacks, harassment, information manipulation, and financial pressure—often with limited resources and little room for error. Guidance alone is not enough, and isolated resilience does not scale.

Real strength emerges when protection is shared: when awareness is collective, signals are pooled, and response is coordinated. When many vulnerable organizations are connected into a trusted ecosystem that can anticipate threats, absorb shocks, and recover together.

(*continued*)

(continued)

Cyberpeace begins there—not in declarations, but in collective protection.

—Inês Narciso, Head of Information Integrity and Resilience, Protect.ngo

PERSPECTIVE: Donors and Foundations—European Climate Foundation

The European Climate Foundation (ECF) is a major philanthropic initiative working to foster the net-zero transition and ensure a healthy, thriving planet for current and future generations. It supports over 700 partner organizations to drive progress towards the goals of the Paris Agreement, promote practical policymaking in response to the climate crisis, and broaden political and public support for climate action. It strives for a positive, people-centered, and socially responsible climate transition in Europe and around the world.

Nonprofit organizations are exposed to growing cybersecurity risks, which threaten their operations and effectiveness. These attacks may be carried out by a range of actors, including state-sponsored groups, financially motivated cybercriminals, and hacktivist organizations targeting specific causes.

In response, the ECF launched the "Building Digital Capacities of Civil Society Organisations" project in 2020. This initiative was primarily focused on improving the cybersecurity skills of its extensive network of grantees, especially in European regions facing higher cybersecurity risks.

The ECF recognized this vulnerability and aimed to fortify the cybersecurity resilience of its partners through this initiative. By equipping these organizations with the necessary skills and knowledge, we are empowering them to better protect their digital assets, safeguard sensitive information, and maintain the trust of their stakeholders.

Starting in 2024, Protect^{ngo} is strengthening the ECF's Building Digital Capacities of Civil Society Organisations program. Through this partnership, the ECF expanded its services to include a wider array of grantees across various regions. We are assured that the Protect^{ngo} initiative is fortifying cybersecurity within our grantee network by offering a tailored approach and access to a platform of seasoned cybersecurity professionals.

Our current Network and Organizational Development initiative benefits greatly from our partnership with Protect^{ngo}. By working together, we're able to help civil society organizations throughout Europe better address cybersecurity challenges, ultimately boosting the resilience of the climate ecosystem.

—Nuno Abano, Cybersecurity Manager, European Climate Foundation

The European Climate Foundation is a philanthropic initiative whose mission is to ensure a safe and healthy future for generations to come. To that end, the Foundation supports hundreds of organizations focusing on reaching the environmental goals set by the Paris Agreement. It advocates for a people-centered, socially responsible ecological transition.

PERSPECTIVE: NGOs—Fondation suisse de déminage

Working in cybersecurity at Fondation suisse de déminage (FSD) is both fun and challenging. Like many NGO IT teams, we didn't start with a solid background in cybersecurity; however, we have gained that knowledge over time. Cyber issues evolve so rapidly that it is important to stay updated: the risks are real, growing, and tied directly to the people and missions we support.

We quickly learned that cybersecurity in an NGO cannot be treated only as a technical problem. Tools are important, but they are never enough on their own; governance, people, and organizational culture are crucial. At FSD, cybersecurity starts with people. People are at the center of everything we do. Our staff is mission-driven and often works under pressure, sometimes in tough environments. Security measures must support our operations and mission delivery, not hinder them. Practical awareness efforts that explain why security matters and how it supports our mission have proven far more effective than rigid rules or fear-based messaging. This is why we run regular cybersecurity awareness training for our staff, followed by phishing simulation exercises, to help ensure that everyone remains informed, engaged, and vigilant.

One of the most important lessons we've learned is the need to stay focused on what truly matters. With limited budgets and small teams, trying to do everything is neither realistic nor helpful. We focus on controls that provide the most value, such as effective identity management, multi-factor authentication (MFA), endpoint protection, reliable backups, and basic monitoring. Cloud-native security features and managed services have transformed our security posture without adding to our operational burden.

Most NGOs can't hire a full in-house security team. We use a hybrid model: a small internal IT team that knows the organization, plus trusted external partners for specialist support. A key factor in this journey has been our partnership with Protect·ngo. It has provided consultation and practical solutions to customize cybersecurity processes for our specific operational needs and to avoid generic models. It has helped us adapt best practices to fit our humanitarian mission, considering our size, resources, and risks. This outside perspective was vital for structuring our approach and strengthening our capabilities without overwhelming our teams.

For FSD, cybersecurity is part of our values. Protecting data and our systems helps protect the people we serve, our staff, and our partners. It's not about perfection. It's about practical steps, shared ownership, and steady improvement.

—Gabriel Anthony Lopre, Microsoft expert, Fondation suisse de déminage

FSD is a Swiss nonprofit operating in regions affected by war and conflict. It focuses on demining the territory for the safety of its population, raising awareness, and supporting accident survivors. More broadly, it aims to protect these communities' safety and dignity.

PERSPECTIVE: Jeroen van den Berg, Municipality of The Hague

The municipality of The Hague and Protect·ngo have a long-standing and fruitful relationship. We have worked together on local projects and have in turn created global impact. This could not have been possible without the passion, the expertise, the network, and the relentless efforts of Protect·ngo. Together, we try to protect those who protect others.

Having Protect·ngo with us in The Hague, in the heart of the international city of peace and justice, has significantly strengthened our cybersecure ecosystem. This ecosystem operates on the borders of local and global efforts. It is about creating local stability and enclosing local knowledge and expertise to truly benefit the advancement of international peace and justice. Protect·ngo plays a critical role in that ecosystem by operationalizing cyber resilience and developing products and services that work.

The close cooperation between Protect·ngo and The Hague started several years ago, when Protect·ngo engaged in a partnership with The Hague Humanity Hub, the Dutch Institute for Vulnerability Disclosure, and the municipality to help local NGOs become more cybersecure. Since 2023, over 200 NGOs in our city have become more cybersecure thanks to the efforts of Protect·ngo. And as of January 2026, together with PEP The Hague, we are now also helping the more than 3,000 nonprofits in our city become more digitally resilient.

In an even more recent highlight, at the beginning of May 2026, the first Protect·ngo event took place as part of the Geneva Cyber Week. Bringing together leaders from civil society organizations, research institutes, and "peace builders" from all over the world, Protect·ngo has managed to

> create a movement of positive change. It has given a face to the daily challenges of NGOs and nonprofits who struggle with keeping their operations, their people, and the people they are trying to protect safe.
>
> We very much look forward to strengthening our cooperation in the near future.
>
> —Jeroen van den Berg, City of The Hague

Impacts on Victims and Targets

Immediate Impacts

When a CSO is attacked, everyone who depends on it is attacked. We must never forget the hundreds of thousands of individuals who inevitably suffer the consequences. They are not collateral damage; they are the real victims of this crisis unfolding before our eyes. Cyberattacks targeting civil society have serious and tangible impacts and a considerable human cost.

Immediately after an attack is when the most concrete impacts are felt: when a CSO is prevented from functioning normally, its beneficiaries are deprived of the aid they should have received. The consequences are significant, regardless of the organization's sector of operation: I will mention examples ranging from access to clean water and geopolitical conflicts to sustainability and blood donation.

Over Time

In addition to these immediate consequences, cyberattacks can have lasting repercussions for CSOs. In the event of a successful attack, they may find themselves locked out of their own systems and unable to access their data. This service interruption can compromise project deadlines. A successful attack can also result in significant financial losses: ransom payments, data breach investigations, system restoration, and potential legal fees are all direct costs. Financial damage, too, can be long-lasting. In 2020, a nonprofit providing aid and shelter to people with limited incomes suffered an attack that, over a period of one month, resulted in more than half a million dollars being extracted from its funds.

In the case of data breaches, disastrous effects can ensue—from identity theft to violated confidentiality. Following an attack against an organization in the sustainability sector, information was leaked to the dark web. It was linked to over 7 million members of the organization, as well as its executive director. It took several months for this information to be discovered and taken off the dark web. There is also the threat of extortion: criminals could potentially exploit breached data to blackmail individuals. The gravest concern, however, lies in repressive regimes with seemingly unlimited power gaining access to the personal data of persons of interest and their families. This could lead to physical attacks, espionage, kidnapping, and even murder. We see this even outside civil society: you might remember the case of Jamal Khashoggi. This journalist and vocal critic of the Saudi government disappeared under mysterious circumstances in 2018 after entering the Saudi Arabian embassy in Istanbul. The investigation showed that he was assassinated, but also that he had previously been tracked using spyware (see Chapter 2). Installing spyware on a person's device is a form of cyber operation that, as in this case, can seriously compromise their physical safety.

We also have to address the harm caused not only to beneficiaries, but to workers and volunteers of targeted organizations. In a report published in 2026 at the request of the City of The

Hague, we found that NGO leaders operate in a particularly risky environment. Since these are people with a certain degree of visibility, the traces they leave in cyberspace can be exploited in phishing attacks, identity theft, or doxxing (disclosure of personal information). CSO leaders are particularly vulnerable to information manipulation campaigns that seek to damage their reputation and that of their organization (see Chapter 2). They are also susceptible to harassment and intimidation that can cross the boundaries of the digital world and threaten their physical integrity. But CSO leaders are not the only ones affected by cyberattacks: staff operating in crisis mode for extended periods of time can suffer dramatic effects as they try to manage the impacts of an attack. It can lead to great distress as well as feelings of guilt for employees who fall victim. The feeling of being vulnerable, exposed to danger, and targeted by people whose identity and objectives are unknown can have serious psychological effects. Employees who click on the wrong link, open the wrong attachment, or fall for an AI-generated voice recording may also find themselves subjected to finger-pointing by colleagues and superiors, and sometimes even dismissed from the organization. In 2024, a report stated that 74% of employees who were victims of cyberattacks in the context of their work faced disciplinary action. This type of reaction from management creates a work environment that is not conducive to transparency in the event of a future cyberattack: in 2025, 39% of workers in the United Kingdom said they would conceal any attack they suffered for fear of reprisals. Though an immediate negative reaction, in a state of panic, is understandable on a human level, it is obviously not the road to go down to contain the repercussions of an attack or to prevent any future incidents. It wouldn't be so frequent if leaders were educated and trained on the subject—that's the kind of measure we advocate for.

Long-Term Consequences

Finally, cyberattacks on nonprofit organizations can have long-term consequences such as reputational damage and loss of trust from stakeholders. In the aftermath of such incidents, some donors can become hesitant to engage with CSOs, fearing for the safety of their financial donations or personal information. The negative perception of nonprofits can divert funds away from them. The loss of donor confidence, coupled with a tarnished public image, can carry long-lasting consequences and block funding streams for years to come.

An organization focusing on blood donations experienced these types of long-term consequences. The CSO suffered a data breach that led to the disclosure of medical information about more than 550,000 individuals. This type of incident impacts donor confidence, which leads to financial loss for the organization. But this case has its own specificity, as in addition to financial donations, this CSO depends on blood donations: a drop in this area can have devastating consequences for beneficiaries. The organization took multiple initiatives to reassure the people who had given their blood and to avoid them being discouraged from doing so again in the future. It was right to take the potential consequences of this attack seriously: loss of trust impacts willingness to help the organization, regardless of the nature of the help.

Recent Developments

The threat landscape for CSOs has evolved even more rapidly in recent years, due to multiple geopolitical and technological developments.

First, the COVID-19 crisis forced CSOs worldwide to accelerate their digital transformation to ensure business continuity. The process had already started: data collection and management have always been critical components of the aid CSOs provide. In recent years, there has been a growing reliance on technology to strengthen programs, engage with beneficiaries, and respond quickly to emergencies. Beyond physical proximity, digitalization allows organizations to develop a virtual presence and offer new services. But this reliance on technology was exacerbated and accelerated by COVID-19, which has created a new vulnerability. During the pandemic and its aftermath, digital development became a core element of CSO strategy. It has become essential for communication, for fundraising, and generally for nonprofits' missions to continue as seamlessly as possible and not be excessively impacted by this pandemic that paralyzed the entire world.

Then came the invasion of Ukraine by Russia in February 2022. Warfare is no longer exclusively kinetic; it is also digital. This is an integral part of the conflict, on both sides, for attack and defense. Cyberattacks also transcend the borders of war, impacting numerous countries in Europe and around the world. A quarterly report by Protect·ngo, which tracked cyberattacks and information manipulation operations over a period of two months (July to September 2023), listed 97 attacks carried out against Ukraine, 13 against the Russian Federation, and 472 incidents in other countries due to the war (Figure 1.2).

Geopolitical conflict has brought on a new type of incident, combining cyberattack and information operations. At Protect·ngo, we call it the "nexus": it's the strategic intersection where cyberattacks and information manipulation combine. In the context of geopolitical conflict, for example, data breaches can be carried out with the intention of espionage. These hybrid attacks are extremely high-impact because of their persistence, coordination, and psychological effects.

At the end of 2022 came the last factor impacting the fast-evolving threat landscape: the rise of artificial intelligence. AI has

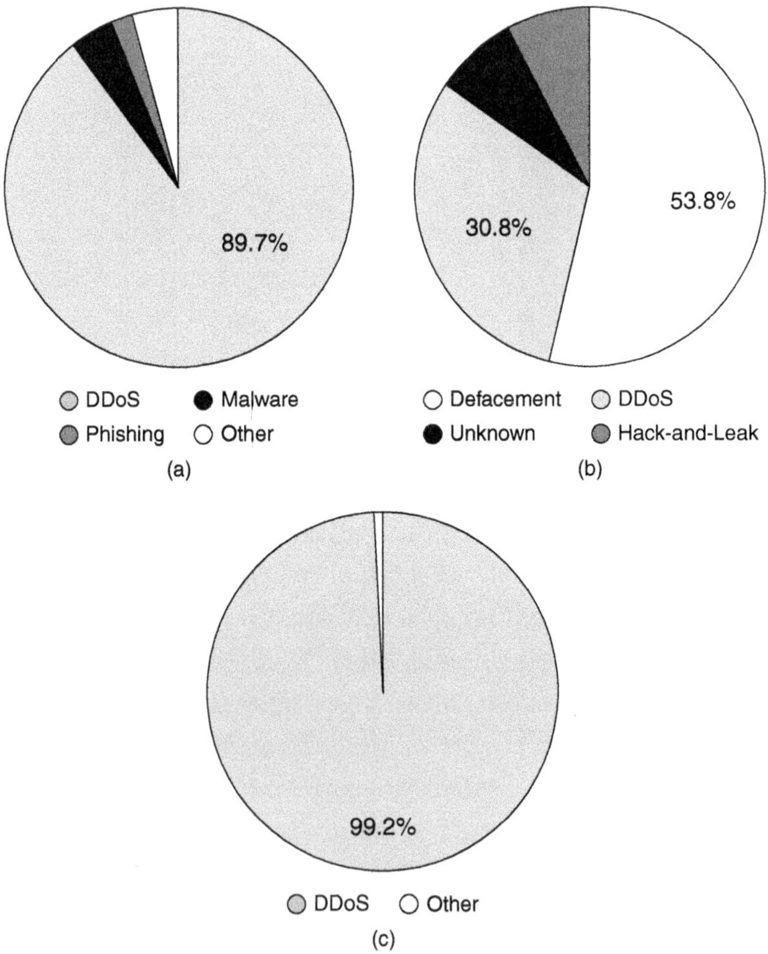

FIGURE 1.2 (a) Types of cyber incidents targeting entities in Ukraine; (b) types of cyber incidents targeting entities in the Russian Federation; (c) types of cyber incidents targeting entities outside the two belligerent states.

Source: Protect·ngo, 2023

been used in cybersecurity since the 1990s, when machine learning and neural networks were applied to spam filtering. But as this technology became a tool for cybersecurity, threat actors also detected its potential. AI-driven cyberattacks are more adaptable to their environment, learn from past attacks, and

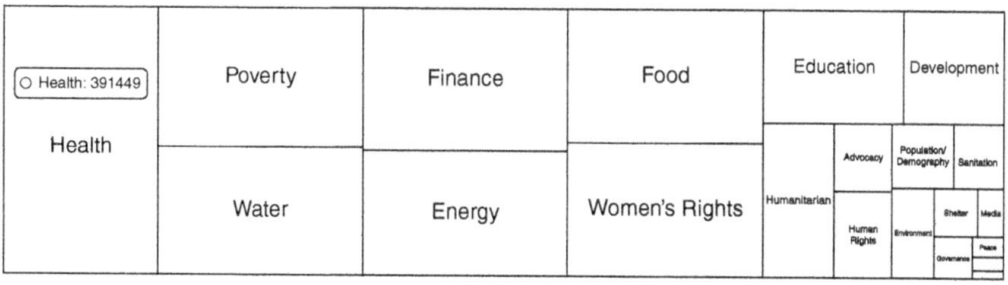

FIGURE 1.3 Relative frequency of incidents per nonprofit sector.
Source: Protect·ngo Tracer, February 2023

improve their capability to hide from antivirus systems. Nowadays, though AI can be a tool for cybersecurity, it is a source of danger for CSOs (Figure 1.3).

In this chapter, I've presented you with multiple cases of cyberattacks, sometimes mentioning them by name, but without providing much detail. In concrete terms, what are they? What triggers them, how do they operate, and what are their consequences? Some seek financial gain; others target the CSO's data; and some simply want to harm its credibility. To anticipate and combat these attacks, it's important to know what we are talking about exactly. If you want to understand how cyberattacks function, and receive specific advice according to their nature and your own range of action, follow me to Chapter 2.

PERSPECTIVE: NGOs—SOS Children's Villages

NGOs have become regular targets of cyberattacks. I learned this firsthand when my organization was hit. As we hold sensitive data on beneficiaries, donors, and partners, and we move money across borders, we are an attractive

(*continued*)

(*continued*)

target. Attackers often assume weak controls and limited capacity. The consequences can be severe: breaches that endanger people, phishing that drains funds, and outages of critical systems.

The "arms race" between new threats and new defenses widens the funding and capacity gap for many NGOs, especially small and midsized ones. Threats evolve fast; thus, controls must be reviewed and improved continuously. But the bigger challenge is governance: treating cybersecurity as a management risk with clear ownership, priorities, and accountability, not as an IT side topic.

What helped my organization improve cyber defense:

Put governance first. Assign one accountable owner for cyber risk, with a clear mandate. Clarify roles across IT, operations, programs, and country offices so responsibility does not fall between teams. Secure leadership backing for tough choices, such as standardization and access limits, and for sufficient budget and capacity. Make the financial case: protecting a ring-fenced cyber budget costs less than recovery.

Build a practical security framework. With project managers and system owners, set mandatory minimum controls, responsibilities, review cycles, and rules for exceptions. Make it mandatory for new projects, procurement, and major changes.

Prioritize the controls that prevent most incidents. Start with multi-factor authentication, least-privilege access, reliable backups, and rapid patching of critical systems. Implement them properly and test them.

Standardize consistently. A fragmented technology landscape increases exposure and cost. Reduce the number of platforms, applications, and configurations. Limit shadow IT.

Manage vendor risk. Require MFA, clear incident-notification timelines, and minimum security standards in contracts. Review critical suppliers regularly, starting with those with the most access or sensitive data.

Collaborate with the NGO community. Join NGO information-sharing groups. Exchange threat patterns, playbooks, and lessons learned. Using volunteer support with care networks such as Protect·ngo or NetHope can help. Peer experience often convinces leadership.

Build staff resilience and audit independently. Train staff regularly on common threats and safe behavior. Arrange independent reviews, from configuration and access audits to targeted penetration tests. External reviewers notice blind spots and provide an objective view of residual risk.

Plan for the day you get hit. Assume an incident will happen—the question is when. Maintain an incident-response playbook and rehearse it so you can act calmly in the first hours. Preselect technical, legal, and communications support, and consider insurance that includes access to such expertise.

—Thomas Rubatscher, SOS Children's Villages

SOS Children's Villages is a nonprofit focused on defending and protecting children all over the world, particularly those suffering from neglect or abandonment. It focuses on prevention, protection, and advocacy to ensure that every child has someone to look over them.

PERSPECTIVE: NGOs

As an IT Manager in a charitable foundation, I often observe that cybersecurity is still perceived by many NGOs as a purely technical topic, secondary to the social mission. This is a mistake. Our organizations handle sensitive data (donors, partners, beneficiaries), rely heavily on public trust, and usually operate with limited resources. Cybersecurity must therefore be approached pragmatically, proportionately, and fully integrated into governance. The following are a few practical recommendations.

Technical Aspects: Focus on the Essentials

There is little value in aiming for complex architectures. It is far more effective to secure the basics properly. Some key fundamentals include:

- Strong authentication (MFA) wherever possible, especially for email, CRM systems, and financial tools
- Password management, through the deployment of a password manager and active monitoring of its proper use
- Endpoint management, including automatic updates and up-to-date antivirus protection
- Regular backups, following the 3-2-1 rule, tested at least once a year
- The principle of least privilege, ensuring users only have access to what is strictly necessary

When it comes to tools, well-configured cloud solutions often provide a higher level of security than poorly maintained in-house systems.

Governance: A Leadership Responsibility

Cybersecurity is a governance issue, not just an IT one. It is essential that senior management understands the risks—financial, legal, and reputational—and validates a clear framework: security policies, incident management procedures, acceptable-use rules, and a cyber risk matrix.

One critical point is defining who makes decisions during a crisis. A ransomware attack on a Friday evening is not the time to debate responsibilities. A simple, well-known, and tested crisis management plan can make all the difference.

Human Resources: Realistic Approaches

Nonprofit organizations usually cannot afford to recruit dedicated cybersecurity experts. A pragmatic approach includes:

- Training a generalist IT manager in core security principles
- Smart outsourcing (annual audits, shared Security Operations Center [SOC] services, on-demand experts)
- Raising staff awareness, which is crucial. After experimenting with traditional group training sessions, we ultimately implemented continuous micro-learning modules integrated into our instant messaging tools

Most incidents start with human error. Investing in awareness and training delivers one of the best returns on investment.

(*continued*)

(*continued*)

Financial Aspects: Think in Terms of Risk

The key question is not "How much does cybersecurity cost?" but "How much would an incident cost?" Data loss, operational downtime, and damage to donor trust can have a major impact.

- I strongly recommend including cybersecurity as a recurring annual budget line—even a modest one—and prioritizing high-impact measures.
- Cyber insurance is also an option that should not be overlooked.

Conclusion

For a foundation, cybersecurity is not a luxury. It is a driver of trust and mission continuity. By staying pragmatic, involving governance, and investing in people as much as in technology, it is possible to achieve a solid level of security that fits our realities.

—Nicolas Haddad, IS Manager and Protect·ngo partner

PERSPECTIVE: NGOs—Peace Direct

Richard Andrew is an IT expert at Peace Direct, an NGO dedicated to resolving conflict and eradicating violence all around the world. He shares his practical advice and basic steps to strengthen CSOs' cybersecurity and digital resilience.

1. **Start with a general cybersecurity assessment through the Protect·ngo cyber volunteer program** (see Chapter 4). This will help identify any immediate risks and gaps in your organization's defenses, as well as steps on how to fix them.

2. **Reduce the attack surface.** Focus on your sign-in and access policies, how your data is stored (structurally), and how your data is shared. Simple steps like maintaining a granular, or "need to know," level of access to your files and sharing files using links instead of attachments will greatly reduce the success of a data breach.
3. **Run a phishing awareness campaign.** Phishing is the most common entry point for breaches. Train your staff in how to spot a phishing email, with examples specific to your organization. Stress that cybersecurity is everyone's responsibility, and not just admin.

—Richard Andrew, Senior Data and Systems Officer, Peace Direct

Peace Direct is an international charity whose mission is to bring an end to violence worldwide. It collaborates with local communities in regions going through war or conflict to bring peaceful resolution and deliver justice for victims.

Sources

Advanced Technology Academic Research Center. "White Paper: Building and Enhancing US Cybersecurity Education and Workforce Development Strategic Initiatives: Advancing National Infrastructure, Capability, and Capacity." August 2024. `https://atarc.org/wp-content/uploads/2024/09/building-and-enhancing-us-cybersecurity-education-and-workforce-development-strategic-initiatives-final-9.10.24-pdf.pdf`

The FinTech Times. "74% of Employees Falling Victim to Phishing Attacks Hit With Disciplinary Actions; Egress Reveals." April 11,

2024.https://thefintechtimes.com/74-of-employees-falling-victim-to-phishing-attacks-hit-with-disciplinary-actions-egress-reveals/?utm

Hall-Jones, Peter. "The Rise and Rise of NGOs." *Global Policy Forum*, May 2006, https://archive.globalpolicy.org/component/content/article/176-general/31937.html

Poireault, Kevin. "Blitz Spear Phishing Campaign Targets NGOs Supporting Ukraine." *InfoSecurity Magazine*, October 24, 2025, https://www.infosecurity-magazine.com/news/blitz-spear-phishing-ngos-ukraine

Protect^ngo. "Cyber Attacks in Times of Conflict – Platform #Ukraine," https://cyberconflicts.protect.ngo

Protect^ngo. "Cyber Dimensions of the Armed Conflict in Ukraine: Quarterly Analysis Report." July–September 2023a. https://cyberconflicts.protect.ngo/report

Protect^ngo. "Protect^ngo Launches 'Humanitarian Cybersecurity Center (HCC)'." February 27, 2023b, https://protect.ngo/news/humanitarian-cybersecurity-center

Protect^ngo. "Cyber-Poor, Target-Rich: The Crucial Role of Cybersecurity in Nonprofit Organizations." March 25, 2024, https://protect.ngo/news/cyber-poor-target-rich-the-crucial-role-of-cybersecurity-in-nonprofit-organizations

Protect^ngo. "Understanding Nexus Operations: Where Cyberattacks and Disinformation Converge." September 1, 2025, https://protect.ngo/news/understanding-nexus-operations-where-cyberattacks-and-disinformation-converge

Woollacott, Emma. "'The Worst Thing an Employee Could Do': Workers Are Covering Up Cyber Attacks for Fear of Reprisal—Here's Why That's a Huge Problem," *ITPro*, July 9, 2025, https://www.itpro.com/security/the-worst-thing-an-employee-could-do-workers-are-covering-up-cyber-attacks-for-fear-of-reprisal-heres-why-thats-a-huge-problem?utm

CHAPTER

2

Resilience: Anatomy of Attacks

July 2023: my phone rings, which, given my lifestyle, is intriguing. Over the years, I have become asynchronous despite myself, not particularly enjoying real-time communication. For years, answering the phone meant being woken up in the middle of the night because of a suicide, a murder, or the discovery of a World War II warhead in a barn. It makes you wary.

On the other end of the line is the head of a CSO whom I have met only 48 hours prior. All my years of public service pale in comparison to the mission of this organization. They are on the ground, everywhere, as a last line of defense to protect children from the dangers they face, from violence to malnutrition.

"RANSOMWARE." The word comes up again and again in the conversation. The organization is paralyzed, and my colleague is distraught. When a CSO falls victim to an attack, operations are interrupted, programs are suspended, and aid cannot be brought to those who need it. It's a particularly vicious type of attack when it targets those who defend people at risk, and who don't necessarily know how to protect themselves. I can sympathize with the loneliness the executive director feels, having to make the right decision in an impossible moment. It feels like everything depends on his response: the safety of his staff, the reputation of his nonprofit, and most of all, the protection of their young beneficiaries all over the world. On top of everything, the response has to be quick. It's a kind of pressure no one should have to endure.

I share some advice: contact the police—of course. Pay the ransom, and indirectly fund the next attack on civil society? Certainly not. Negotiate? Maybe, depending on the attacker and their motives. I list a series of actions to be taken. In a crisis, it's reassuring to know what to do, to be able to follow a proven methodology. To feel some semblance of control over the ship in the storm.

Unfortunately, ransomware attacks are far from being the only ones targeting CSOs, and these various threats are neither rare nor random: they happen everywhere, all the time. Attacks of all kinds impact all sectors of civil society, including health, social services, and education (Figure 2.1). In this chapter, I will explore the four most common types of attacks against CSOs and one technique with a unique status, before delving into the increasingly prevalent role played by the emerging technology of artificial intelligence (AI). More importantly, I will list concrete and practical solutions that you can put in place to protect yourself from each of these types of attacks.

Though it's important for as many people as possible to be educated on this subject, cybersecurity is a field of knowledge in its own right, and a highly specialized one at that. So, if you have

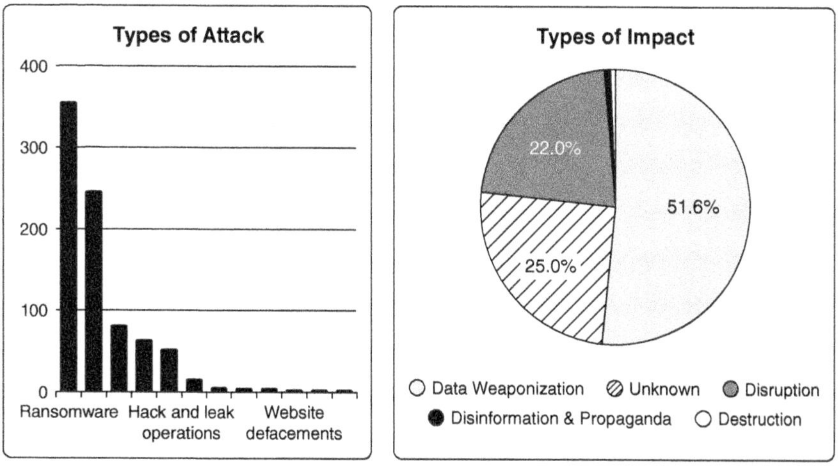

FIGURE 2.1 Types of attacks targeting nonprofits, and their impacts.
Source: Protect^{ngo} Tracer, February 2026

any doubts, any hesitations, or if you simply don't want to go about strengthening your organization's digital resilience by yourself, I suggest joining the Protect^{ngo} cyber volunteer program. Thousands of cyber volunteers are here to go through this process with you, for free. If you need any advice, I invite you to visit `www.protect.ngo`.

Phishing: The Most Prevalent Threat

What Is It?

In order to understand the different cyberattacks carried out against civil society, we cannot avoid focusing on phishing as a criminal modus operandi. While phishing, in itself, is considered a cyberattack, it is not profitable. It's a point of entry: it allows criminals to access an organization's system and its data. Only later will other attacks be deployed. A phishing operation is never an end in itself: it is a means of accessing elements which are insufficiently protected.

When it comes to phishing operations, they usually consist of fraudulent emails. The email appears to have been sent from a trusted organization (government, partner CSO. . .). The recipient is encouraged to click on a link or open an attachment; this is the point at which the safety of the system is compromised. The criminals could then, for example, steal data—passwords or banking information—or install malicious software (malware) on the computer.

Just like other practices I will mention (such as CEO fraud), phishing is a form of social engineering. By this, we mean the manipulation of individuals, leading them to act in a way that is beneficial to the attacker: click a link or open an attachment, reveal a password, or approve a wire transfer.

What Is the Danger to Civil Society?

Phishing is particularly effective when the staff of the targeted nonprofit isn't sufficiently trained to spot and bypass fraudulent emails—which, taking into account the limited budget CSOs are able to dedicate to their cybersecurity and how AI accelerates the phishing capabilities of attackers, poses a grave danger. Employees and volunteers working for CSOs are not always aware of the dangers, and even if they are, they don't always know how to identify a fraud attempt or have the necessary reflexes to avoid it. Cybercriminals exploit this gap in knowledge or training, and the consequences can be disastrous. For example, following a phishing attack, in addition to financial theft, filtered data can be shared or sold to allow other actors to infiltrate the system, or stolen credentials can be used for email surveillance or to launch new phishing campaigns.

Data breaches are one of the main dangers emerging from phishing attacks against civil society. Under the leadership of the City of The Hague, in the context of its CyberSecure program, we partnered in 2024 with The Hague Humanity Hub, Stichting the Shadowserver Foundation Europe, and the Connect2Trust Foundation. We analyzed the risks posed to Dutch NGOs by data theft, one of the main consequences of phishing attacks. Our conclusions show that between October 2023 and October 2024, 43% of the 30 surveyed NGOs fell victim to credential theft. In each of these cases, their credentials were published on the dark web, on forums frequented by hackers. These results highlight the substantial and permanent risk that CSOs face regarding the safety of their data and operations (Figure 2.2).

Example: In 2023, an American nonprofit that strives to combat hunger received an email seemingly sent by a construction company with which they were doing business. The email contained a fake invoice for a service provided by the construction company; the nonprofit, not doubting the veracity of the email or invoice, wired the corresponding amount. Unfortunately, it was a phishing attack. Cybercriminals had intercepted exchanges between the nonprofit and the construction company

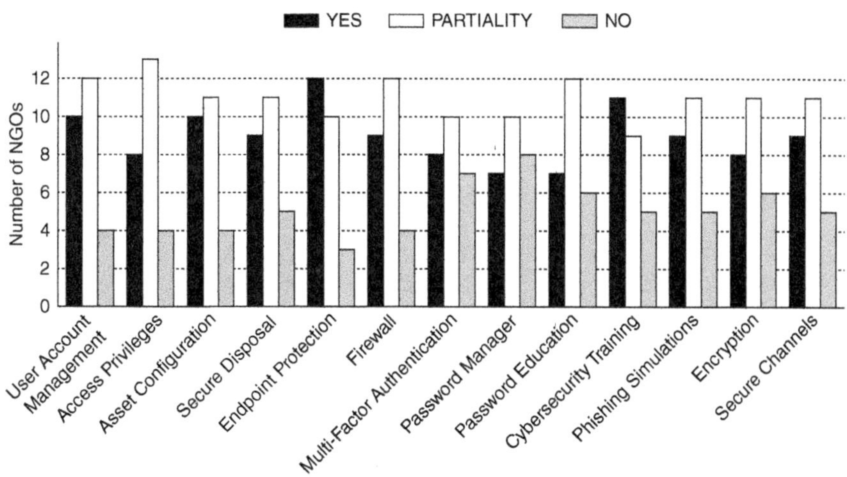

FIGURE 2.2 NGO compliance levels in terms of cyber protection.

Source: The Hague Humanity Hub, Protect·ngo, Stichting the Shadowserver Foundation Europe, and Connect2Trust Foundation, 2024

and had replicated them in order to impersonate the company as convincingly as possible. The organization was cheated, in total, out of $923,000. This amount is all the more significant in a sector in which each dollar counts, and it damaged the nonprofit's reputation in the eyes of the public.

What About Society as a Whole?

The results of phishing attacks can take on gigantic proportions, notably on a geopolitical level, as they can be a tool for cyberespionage. Let's go back to the 2022 invasion of Ukraine by Russia. As was mentioned earlier, this war has placed cyberattacks front and center when it comes to geopolitical conflict. In the context of the war, cyberattacks are not only aimed at the two belligerent countries. Some of them target other countries—the threat extending to states that participate through military or humanitarian aid, financial sanctions, or political support (Figure 2.3). In fact, countries within NATO, which provide aid to Ukraine, are particularly wary of criminal organizations affiliated with the Russian state. Since 2022, some 13 cyberattacks have been attributed to them, with varying degrees of certainty; at least 8 of these attacks aimed to extract data or conduct espionage. They allow the country behind the attacks to exfiltrate data relating to aid provided, future operations, and also simply to demonstrate the state's ability to infiltrate systems in order to intimidate and deter victims from continuing to extend their support.

Understanding the Issue: How to Spot a Phishy Email

There is no standard template for a phishing email. They sometimes look dramatic, and sometimes they blend into the routine. They can be long, short, with typos, or with perfect spelling and design. Learning to spot them is less about technical expertise and more about developing a habit of calm attention.

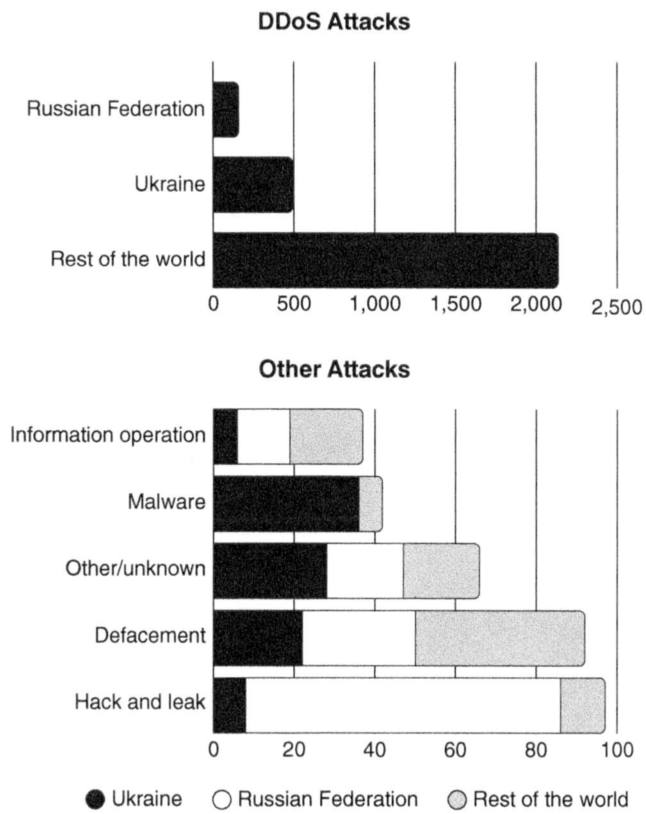

FIGURE 2.3 Types of attacks deployed against organizations, by country of organization.

Source: Adapted from The Hague Humanity Hub (2024)

- Urgency is the biggest red flag.

  Phishing emails almost always try to rush you. They often claim something bad will happen unless you act immediately:
  - Funding, access, or services will be lost.
  - An account will be suspended.
  - A payment has failed.
  - A document needs immediate review.
  - A deadline is about to expire.

Urgency is not accidental. It is meant to override your judgment. When an email pushes you to act *now*, pause. Legitimate organizations rarely punish you for taking a moment to verify a request.

- The sender feels unfamiliar, or oddly familiar.

  Be especially careful when:
  - You receive an email from someone for the first time.
  - The sender is someone you rarely hear from.
  - The message comes from outside your organization.
  - The name looks familiar, but something feels off.

  Email addresses can be forged. A message may appear to come from a colleague, partner, or manager, even when it does not. Familiarity should never replace verification.

- The messages contain generic greetings and vague language.

  Messages that start with "Dear user," "Dear colleague," or "Dear team" deserve extra scrutiny. Organizations that genuinely work with your CSO usually know who you are. Phishing emails often stay vague so they can be sent to many people at once.

- There are small mistakes and inconsistencies.

  Spelling or grammar mistakes are worth noticing, but so are subtler issues such as:
  - Unusual wording or phrasing
  - Formatting that differs from past messages
  - A tone that doesn't match previous emails
  - Messages that feel unusually formal or unusually casual

  These details alone do not prove an email is malicious but, combined with other signs, they matter.

- The email address does not match the sender.

Always look at the full email address, not just the name. A message may claim to be from a trusted organization but be sent from an unrelated email domain. If the organization name and the email address do not align, treat the message with caution.

- The email requests sensitive information.

  Phishing emails often ask for things they should not: passwords or verification codes, personal details, donor information, internal documents, etc. Legitimate organizations rarely request sensitive information by email.

- The email includes links that ask you to sign in.

  A common phishing tactic is to send you to a fake website that looks real. Before clicking on any link, hover over it and read the full address carefully. Check whether it clearly belongs to the organization it claims to represent.

- The email includes unexpected attachments.

  Be cautious with attachments you were not expecting, even if they appear to come from someone you know. Files can contain harmful software that installs itself silently when opened.

- The email includes offers that sound too good to be true.

  Unexpected prizes, refunds, grants, or urgent opportunities should trigger skepticism. If something sounds too good to be true, it probably is, especially if it arrives without context.

Taking Action: Best Practices

How can we avoid falling victim to a phishing attack, this threat that looms so heavily on civil society? For each type of attack we will explore, it's mainly about putting in place a certain culture and habits on an organizational level. Here are a few pieces of advice:

1. Train regularly and practically.

   Organize regular training sessions to raise awareness among staff members (this goes for all types of attacks). Short, practical awareness sessions help keep risks visible. Training should focus on real scenarios staff encounter every day: emails from partners, donors, platforms, or colleagues. Connecting cyber risks to the safety of beneficiaries and the organization's mission makes the issue tangible.

2. Favor an open security culture in which each staff member feels free to ask questions if they have doubts.

   The most effective protection is an open environment where staff feel comfortable asking for a second opinion. No one should feel embarrassed about saying, "This email feels strange, can you look at it with me?" Phishing succeeds when people feel rushed or isolated.

3. Learn from real examples.

   Create a shared file in which each employee can add screenshots of phishing emails they have received so that everyone can refer to them. This creates a collective memory of threats and helps everyone recognize patterns faster.

4. Protect accounts with an extra step.

   Activate multi-factor authentication (MFA) on all CSO accounts. MFA involves checking an additional factor that only the real user has. This means that even if a password is stolen, attackers cannot easily access the account. This single measure dramatically reduces risk.

5. Reduce exposure before emails arrive.

   Many CSOs rely heavily on email to communicate with donors, partners, volunteers, and communities. This makes anti-phishing filters on email inboxes a practical and important layer of defense.

   Anti-phishing email filters can automatically block or flag suspicious messages before they reach staff inboxes. These systems look for common warning signs such as misleading links, unfamiliar sender addresses, unexpected attachments, or messages designed to create false urgency.

   For organizations with limited technical capacity, these tools are especially valuable because they reduce the number of risky emails that staff must evaluate under pressure. While no filter is perfect, even basic email protection can significantly lower exposure and give teams more breathing room to make careful decisions.

6. Slow down as a rule.

   Encourage staff to pause before clicking, downloading, or replying, especially when an email creates urgency. Taking a moment to verify is often enough to prevent harm. It's what the Take9 initiative raises awareness about: for more information on this, check out their perspective at the end of this section.

Learning from It: What to Do if a Phishing Attack Happens

Phishing is not a personal failure. Even experienced professionals fall victim to well-designed attacks, especially when working under pressure or with limited time. What matters most is how quickly and calmly the organization responds.

In the first minutes after a suspected phishing incident, the priority is not to assign blame or solve everything at once. The goal is to contain potential harm, preserve information, and alert others who may be affected.

1. Understand what occurred.

   Determine what action was taken: Was a link clicked? Were credentials entered? Was a file downloaded? This helps assess the level of risk and next steps.

2. Alert others immediately.

   Inform colleagues or managers as soon as possible so they can avoid similar messages. Phishing campaigns often target multiple people at once, and early warnings can prevent further damage. Even a short message like "I received a suspicious email; please be cautious" can make a difference.

3. Follow internal procedures.

   If your organization has guidelines for incidents, use them. If not, this experience highlights the importance of creating a few simple response steps that everyone understands and can follow.

4. Secure accounts and devices.

   Change any affected passwords using official websites, not links in emails. If malware is suspected, disconnect the device from the Internet and run a full security scan.

5. Inform affected external parties.

   If donor, partner, or beneficiary information may have been exposed, inform them promptly. Transparency helps others protect themselves.

6. Stay alert for follow-up harm.

   Monitor for unusual account activity, unexpected financial transactions, or identity misuse. Phishing is often the first step in a broader attack.

7. Report the incident.

   Reporting phishing attacks helps protect not only your organization, but others in your ecosystem. When attackers reuse the same messages across multiple organizations, early reports can prevent wider harm.

   If the phishing email impersonates a known organization or platform (such as an email provider, donor platform, or bank), report it directly to them. Many organizations have dedicated channels to investigate misuse of their name or systems.

   Where possible, also report the incident to national or regional cyber incident reporting bodies. Even if no immediate action follows, these reports contribute to broader awareness and can support collective defenses over time.

   If reporting feels overwhelming, start small: save the email, note what happened, and share the information with trusted partners or networks. As mentioned before, collective visibility is also a form of protection.

8. Turn the incident into learning.

   After the immediate risk has passed, go back to *point 1* and take time to reflect on what happened. What made the message convincing? Where did confusion arise? Sharing these lessons openly helps strengthen collective awareness and reduces the likelihood of similar incidents in the future.

ATTACK PROFILE: Phishing

Understanding the Issue: How to Spot a Phishy Email

- Creates urgency or pressure to act immediately
- Comes from an unfamiliar or unexpected sender
- Uses generic greetings or vague language
- Contains unusual wording, tone, or formatting
- Sender name and email address do not match
- Asks for passwords or sensitive information
- Includes links asking you to sign in
- Has unexpected attachments
- Promises rewards, refunds, or opportunities

Taking Action: Best Practices

- Pause before clicking, downloading, or replying.
- Verify requests through another channel.
- Encourage staff to ask for a second opinion.
- Train regularly using real-life examples.
- Share suspicious emails internally.
- Enable multi-factor authentication (MFA).
- Use email filtering and anti-phishing tools.

Learning from It: What to Do if a Phishing Attack Happens

- Stay calm and act quickly.
- Identify what action was taken.
- Alert colleagues immediately.

- Change affected passwords safely.
- Secure devices and run scans.
- Follow internal response steps.
- Inform affected partners or donors.
- Monitor for follow-up activity.
- Report the phishing attempt.
- Share lessons learned.

Report an incident: `https://incident.protect.ngo`

Useful resources:

The Take9 campaign: `https://pausetake9.org`

Take9 is a public service campaign launched by Craig Newmark Philanthropies—an important donor in the non-profit cybersecurity network—which also acts as a coalition of cybersecurity organizations. It encourages individuals to pause for 9 seconds and engage in critical thinking before clicking a link, opening an attachment, or acting in any way that might put them or their organization in harm's way.

The Global Cyber Alliance Toolkits: `https://gcatoolkit.org/smallbusiness/prevent-phishing-and-malware`

PERSPECTIVE: Cyber Civil Society—Take9

NGOs play a crucial role in fulfilling the gap between community needs and public policy, often providing support, resources, and advocacy needed to strengthen civil society and democracy. While filling these critical gaps, they address the needs of local communities and support those who are most at risk within the ecosystem. As pillars of our societal well-being and holders of civic trust, data, and engagement, they're increasingly targeted by state-sponsored actors through cyberattacks and threats—especially given that many of them lack the resources, skills, and financial means to prioritize cybersecurity within their systems. It's critical that we address this gap and support NGOs, as cyberattacks have the ability to disrupt their vital, potentially life-saving, work and impact the already vulnerable communities that they serve.

There is a range of low-cost cybersecurity measures that can be implemented by NGOs to improve their digital hygiene, including implementing MFA, secure backups, password managers or passkeys, secure communications, automatic updates, and adopting "zero-trust" principles that ensure verification happens throughout their internal systems—along with building capacity among their employees through scenario-based training, reviewing security processes for third-party or vendor management, and creating protocols for hypothetical scenarios, all of which will also greatly improve protection and preparedness against attacks.

Since national resilience depends on the security of NGOs, we additionally need collaborative and industry-based approaches to ensure they get the support they need to implement these technical measures and increase their capacity. Additional support from the cybersecurity community through volunteer-led or corporate responsibility initiatives, such as the Cyber Resilience Corps [see Chapter 4], can support gaps in resources and capacity in scalable and meaningful ways.

We also need to create a culture of security awareness for society and NGOs, to ensure individuals are playing their part to implement safer systems and prevent potential attacks. As a public service awareness campaign created by Craig Newmark Philanthropies and supported by Aspen Digital, Take9 (`pausetake9.org`) encourages individuals to slow down and take 9 seconds to think critically when approached with something out of the ordinary online. While encouraging the power of the pause while threat actors are preying on a sense of urgency, the campaign equips individuals with easy-to-use and accessible resources that help them confidently protect themselves and their communities. Since launching in 2024, Take9 has reached millions of consumers as it continues to scale behavioral awareness around cybersecurity threats and lasting behavioral change.

In a time when over half of all NGOs are experiencing cyberattacks, many of which are persistent and continuously increasing, it's imperative that we support these spaces by preparing them with tools to strengthen their security, supporting them through collaborative initiatives, and amplifying campaigns to increase security awareness.

—Amira Dhalla, Director of Cyber Civil Defense, Aspen Digital

Ransomware: A Growing Threat to Civil Society

What Is It?

In order to understand ransomware, we have to understand malware. Malware is a type of software made to damage, destruct, or disrupt computer systems. It could be, for example, a virus that prevents the system from functioning.

Ransomware is a type of malware. During a ransomware attack, a hacker encrypts their victim's data or files, rendering them inaccessible. This is generally done through a malicious attachment, the download of infected software, or by taking advantage of vulnerabilities in the system. After encrypting the files on the victim's computer, the hacker displays a ransom note on the screen or leaves a text file detailing the instructions for the payment, usually through cryptocurrency.

What Is the Danger to Civil Society?

A ransomware attack can completely paralyze a nonprofit organization. Since access to its information system is prevented, its mission suffers and can, in the most severe cases, be completely interrupted. The ransom note leads to a crucial dilemma: leaders may be tempted to pay the requested sum in order to resume their work as fast as possible. But this is precisely the trap: the organization will simply have lost a considerable amount of money that could have been invested in the services it offers, and the attacker will come out richer and stronger for future attacks. Furthermore, paying the ransom does not preclude a future attack. This type of attack has a particularly high recurrence rate, since once vulnerabilities are identified in a nonprofit's system, they are exploited, either again by the same attackers or by new criminals following the dissemination of information.

In the winter of 2020, an employee of a Geneva-based CSO, which provides services to other local and international associations, accidentally opened a PDF file containing malware, which had been received via email. This led to the encryption of data on their computer before spreading to the organization's server. On this server was crucial financial and accounting information, as well as personal employee data. The criminals who led the attack demanded a considerable amount of money, in Bitcoin, for the data to be decrypted. The CSO leaders decided not to pay. They were hoping to get their data back thanks to automatic backup; however, the system had not been recently updated and didn't contain the data for the past few weeks, which was lost as a result.

This attack had multiple consequences for the organization: first, the loss of data as well as the time and effort invested to try to get it back. It also impacted budget planning and led to unexpected spending in order to compensate for the organization's lack of cybersecurity. The server as well as one of the computers were temporarily disabled, and the employee who fell victim to the attack as well as their colleagues suffered psychological distress.

Following this incident, leaders of the organization became aware of its cybersecurity gap and invested in cyber insurance as well as training for their staff.

What About Society as a Whole?

Ransomware attacks are particularly harmful when they impact civil society, but it isn't their only victim. Their frequency is increasing at a stable pace that is expected to continue over the next few years, notably because of the use of AI and the expansion of dark web markets. These are tools that allow individuals to engage in criminal activity without requiring extensive knowledge. This phenomenon is amplified by the rise of the "ransomware-as-a-service" model, through which criminals share ransomware with other attackers in exchange for a slice of the profits.

In October 2025, Protect·ngo published a report about the ransomware phenomenon and the involvement of state or state-affiliated actors. The report registers 2,753 cases of ransomware attacks between 2020 and 2025. It covers 21 impacted sectors in 99 countries and attributes the incidents to 162 different actors (Figure 2.4).

The results of the study show that the United States is the most frequently attacked country, suffering 54% of incidents, followed by the United Kingdom and Australia (Figure 2.5). This disproportionate targeting is partially attributable to the fact that American companies operate in some of the world's most profitable sectors (health, energy, technology). The most highly targeted sectors are health, public administration, and education (Figure 2.6). As for the geographical regions from which the

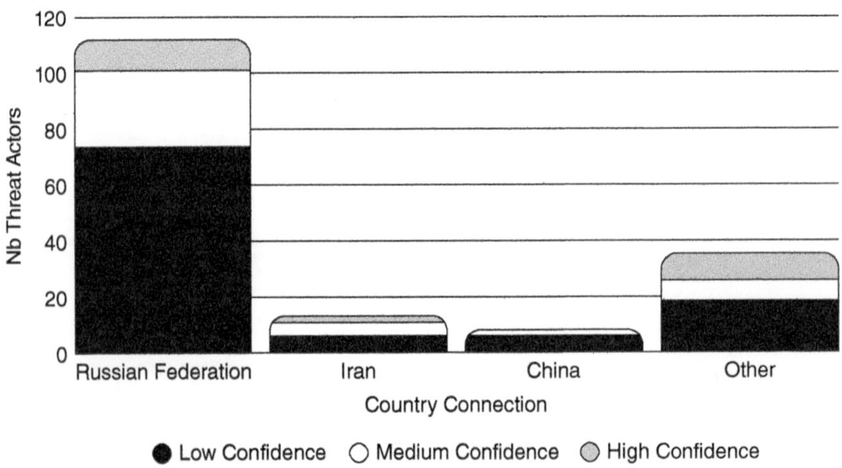

FIGURE 2.4 Country distribution of ransomware threat actors.
Source: Protect·ngo, 2025

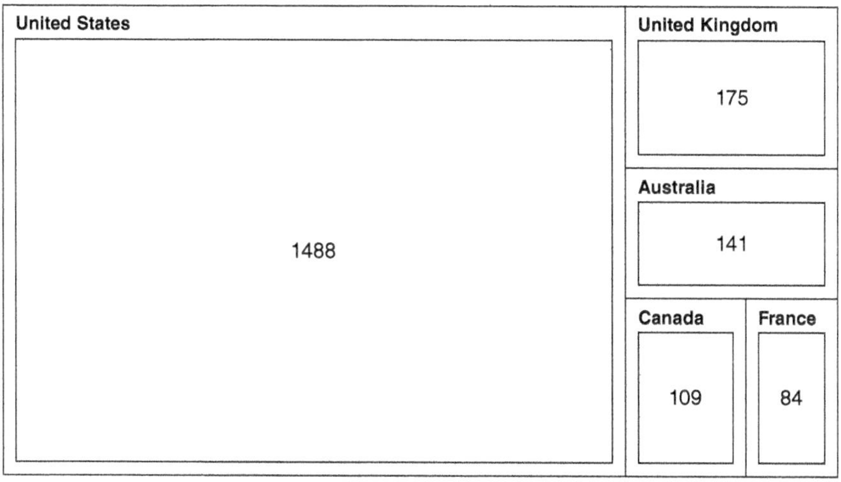

FIGURE 2.5 The five most frequently targeted countries in terms of ransomware attacks.

Source: Protect·ngo, 2025

attacks are deployed, we find the Russian Federation at the top of the list, followed by Iran and China. The links are presented with different degrees of confidence and do not necessarily imply affiliation with a state with complete certainty.

The consequences of ransomware attacks largely surpass financial cost. Low- to middle-income countries are particularly vulnerable to the destructive force of these attacks. In the case of operations involving state actors, such as those analyzed in the report cited earlier, they are considered transnational crimes. The national and international response to these incidents must follow the rapid evolution of the ecosystem in which they exist. Unfortunately, the measures taken by law enforcement to this day have had limited global impact. They remain insufficient for justice to be done and for reparations to be obtained for the victims.

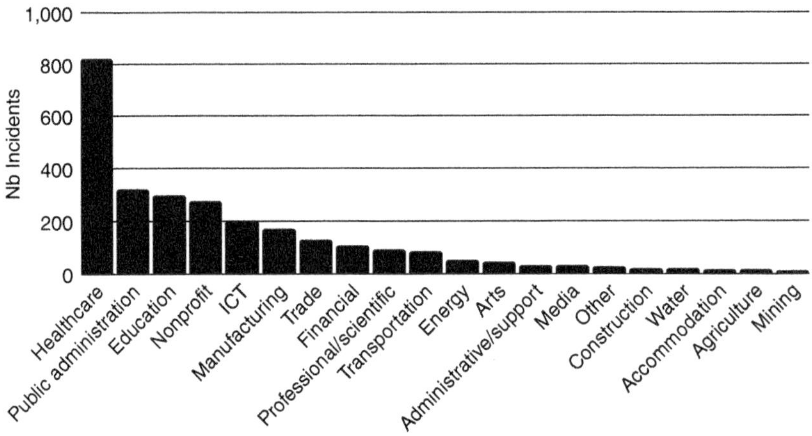

FIGURE 2.6 Distribution of nonprofit sectors targeted by ransomware attacks, 2020–2025.

Source: Protect·ngo, 2025

Understanding the Issue: How to Spot a Ransomware Attack

Ransomware attacks can take many different forms. They may arrive quietly or all at once, and their impact can range from minor disruption to a full organizational crisis. The way an attack enters a system often determines how the ransomware behaves and how much damage it can cause.

The best moment to stop a ransomware attack is early, before it fully takes hold. At first, many attacks are automated, simple attempts to get a foot in the door. Once a human attacker steps in, using proven tools and step-by-step playbooks, stopping the attack becomes much harder. Cutting the power early is far easier than putting out a full fire.

1. Signs of initial access.

   One of the most common ways ransomware enters an organization is through suspicious emails and phishing attempts. These messages are designed to trick people into clicking a link or opening an attachment that secretly installs malicious software. Even emails that look ordinary or appear to come from a trusted source can be dangerous (see the previous section on phishing for more detail).

Another common entry point is poorly protected remote access (RDP). Many organizations use remote access tools that allow staff or IT support to log into a computer from another location, as if they were physically present. Remote Desktop is one common example. If these tools rely on weak passwords, shared accounts, or lack additional security checks, attackers can break in by guessing or stealing login details. Once inside, they may quietly explore the system, install malicious software, or prepare a ransomware attack without being noticed. Because this activity often looks like a normal login, it can be difficult to detect in the early stages.

2. Signs of system compromise.

   One of the clearest warning signs of ransomware is when files suddenly change names or acquire unusual extensions. This usually means the files have been encrypted by the attacker and cannot be opened without a special key.

   Suspicious scheduled tasks are another warning to look out for. Attackers also often set up automated tasks on compromised systems. These scheduled tasks allow their access to survive system reboots and help them remain hidden and persistent over time.

   Another warning sign is the unexpected installation of remote access software. If these tools appear on a system without a clear, legitimate reason, it may indicate that someone is maintaining remote control of the computer.

3. Privilege abuse and credential theft.

   In many organizations, there is a central system that manages user accounts, controlling who can log in, which computers they can use, and what information they are allowed to access. Active Directory is a common example of such a system. Unusual activity in the organization's central account system is a sign to look out for. Gaining control here is like getting the master key to the building: it allows wide access across the network.

A potential warning sign of a ransomware attack is unusual attempts to access multiple systems using existing usernames and passwords. Attackers often try to steal these login details directly from a computer's memory to gain wider access across the network. Early signs might include users being locked out of accounts, unexpected logins from unusual locations, or alerts from security systems about repeated login attempts.

The presence of other malware is another warning sign, especially when it is detected that an attacker is trying to escalate their privileges and gain deeper access within the organization.

4. Exploring the network and spreading to other computers.

   One early warning sign is unusual activity on your network, such as systems scanning other computers or services. Once inside, attackers often explore the network to see what systems exist and which ones are valuable. This is similar to walking through hallways and checking which doors are unlocked.

   Another sign is the misuse of built-in administration tools. If administration tools are being used in unexpected ways, moving between computers or running commands remotely, this can indicate that someone is trying to expand their control without being noticed.

   The appearance of specialized security testing software, which is normally used for testing security, can also be a warning. While legitimate in certain contexts, its presence on systems without a clear reason often points to an attacker carrying out advanced steps to take over the network.

5. Disabling defenses.

   A common step before a ransomware attack is to weaken or shut down security protections. If antivirus or other security tools are suddenly turned off or removed, it may indicate that an attacker has gained high-level access and is preparing to launch the attack. In some cases, attackers use special software designed specifically to disable or bypass these protections, which is a serious warning sign that the situation is escalating.

6. Data theft and external communication.

   One warning sign is unusual outgoing Internet activity, such as sudden spikes in data being sent outside the organization. Attackers often rely on legitimate tools, like built-in file transfer services or popular cloud platforms, to move this data out quietly. Because these tools are commonly used for everyday work, this activity can blend in with normal behavior and be harder to spot.

Taking Action: Best Practices

Malware infiltrates a system, most often, when a person clicks a dangerous link. To avoid this and to limit its consequences, several habits can be put in place.

1. Keep software up to date.

   Close the door before they enter. Ransomware often exploits vulnerabilities in outdated software—think of these flaws like unlocked doors or broken windows. Operating systems and applications release updates can help to fix these issues. Installing updates regularly on computers, phones, and programs is one of the simplest and most effective ways to reduce risk. While it may feel like a minor chore, keeping software current is like locking up before leaving the office: it prevents attackers from walking in uninvited.

2. Protect accounts with multi-factor authentication (MFA).

   Many ransomware attacks begin when attackers gain access to email accounts or internal platforms through stolen or guessed passwords. Multi-factor authentication adds an extra layer of security. Even if someone knows a password, they still need a second verification (like a code sent to a phone or generated by an app). For small teams with limited resources, MFA offers a huge security boost with minimal effort.

3. Use strong passwords and manage them carefully.

   Weak or reused passwords remain one of the main causes of ransomware infections. Using long, unique, and hard-to-guess passwords reduces the chances of unauthorized access. Limiting login attempts so accounts lock temporarily after several failed tries also helps. Clear password policies can strengthen security across teams, especially when staff or volunteers come and go.

4. Restrict user privileges and maintain good account hygiene.

   Restricting user privileges means ensuring that each staff member can only access the information and systems they need for their role. This reduces the potential damage if an account is compromised. Regularly reviewing accounts and systematically deleting those of employees who leave the organization is equally important.

5. Protect email, the most common entry point.

   Email is still the favorite gateway for ransomware. Malicious attachments, infected links, or messages that create a false sense of urgency are common tactics. Email filtering systems can detect suspicious messages before they reach staff, blocking known threats and phishing attempts (more information in the "phishing" section). For CSOs handling sensitive information or working in high-risk contexts, this extra layer of protection can make a crucial difference.

6. Be aware of unverified links and attachments.

   A simple but powerful rule: don't click links or open files from unknown sources. Many attacks start with a single click. Once ransomware enters a system, it can lock files and spread rapidly.

7. Protect devices, not just the network.

   Laptops, phones, and tablets are essential for civil society work but can also be weak points. Using antimalware programs helps detect threats and isolate compromised devices. Limiting which applications can be installed also prevents malicious programs from taking hold. These steps reduce opportunities for attacks even if they cannot fully stop a determined intruder.

8. Make frequent backups and use separate systems.

   Backups are your insurance. Regularly saving data in separate, disconnected locations means you can recover files without paying ransoms or rebuilding everything from scratch. Backups should be made regularly and stored in separate, disconnected locations, because many ransomware variants try to delete accessible backups. Combining a cloud backup with a physical one, and ensuring they are only used after the problem is eliminated, significantly increases recovery options.

9. Use secure networks when connecting from public spaces.

   Working from cafes, airports, or shared spaces is a common practice for most of us. However, public Wi-Fi networks can be exploited by attackers to intercept data or introduce malware. Using a virtual private network (VPN) protects information by encrypting the communication between the device and the Internet. This makes it harder for third parties to access information, even on open networks.

10. Stop ransomware from phoning home.

    Having a firewall, proxy, or intrusion detection system (IDS/IPS) helps spot and block suspicious connections. Today, many ransomware variants try to communicate with a remote server to receive instructions—this is called Command and Control (C&C or C2). Even if the ransomware slips past antivirus software, a firewall, proxy, or IDS acts like a security gate, stopping it from "phoning home" to its server and preventing it from carrying out further malicious actions.

11. Periodically review weak points.

    Check which devices and services are exposed to the Internet and address any vulnerabilities. Identifying issues before attackers do is key to preventing an incident.

12. Adopt a "zero trust" mindset.

    Traditionally, many organizations trusted everything happening within their network. However, ransomware can spread quickly once inside a network. A "zero trust" approach assumes that no user or device is automatically safe, even within the organization. Limiting access to the minimum needed and regularly reviewing permissions reduces potential damage.

13. Promote a culture of caution.

    Technical measures help, but habits matter just as much. Staff should feel comfortable verifying messages before interacting with them, especially in environments with volunteers or temporary staff. Collective vigilance is one of the strongest defenses against ransomware.

Learning from It: How to Respond to a Ransomware Attack

Even with strong defenses, no organization is completely immune. Knowing how to respond is just as important as preventing an attack.

1. Immediately isolate the affected device.

   The first step is to prevent the attack from spreading. This usually involves disconnecting the affected device from the network right away. In some cases, shutting down the device may also be the best move, especially if advised by technical staff. Make sure to:

   - Unplug network cables and disconnect shared devices such as printers.
   - Turn off Wi-Fi in the affected area, since wireless connections can let ransomware jump to other devices.
   - Disconnect external or shared storage devices immediately. Ransomware can hide there and later spread to other computers.

   Ransomware can infect certain devices and later spread from there to other computers. For this reason, it is advisable to assume these devices are compromised until they have been properly examined and cleaned. Think of this step like putting up a quarantine fence: anything inside might be infected, so it stays separated until it's safely checked and cleaned.

2. Identify the type of attack.

   Once the immediate threat is contained, try to figure out what kind of ransomware you're dealing with. Look for clues such as the ransom message, changes to file names or extensions, or instructions left on the screen by the attackers.

   This information is crucial for deciding what to do next. For some types of ransomware, solutions already exist, including decryption keys that can recover files without paying the ransom. To make this possible, don't rush into action. Preserve all information for specialized personnel, whether internal or external, to analyze. Early identification also helps you avoid steps that could make the situation worse.

3. Remove the malware at the right time.

   Removing the malicious software is necessary, but timing is key. Attempting to delete the ransomware before isolating the device or identifying the type of attack can make it easier for the infection to spread or can cause important information to be lost.

   Once the device is safely isolated and the attack understood, removing the malware helps prevent further infections, even if the device remains offline. This step usually requires specialized technical support, especially to ensure the system is truly clean and safe to use again.

4. Recover information and restore operations.

   After the attack is contained, the next step is to recover data and resume your organization's work. How quickly this happens depends largely on whether you have recent backups.

Backups may be stored in cloud services or on internal systems, as long as they can be accessed from a device other than the one affected. Make sure credentials for backups are secure and not only on the compromised device. Frequent backups act like a safety net: if files are lost, the damage is limited and recovery is faster.

5. Do not pay the ransom.

   Being locked out of critical files can feel like a ticking clock, and paying the ransom may seem like a quick fix. But it is not recommended. As criminals, the attackers' only interest is obtaining money, not keeping promises. There is no guarantee they will restore access, and paying marks the organization as a willing target, increasing the risk of future attacks. Refusing to pay not only protects the organization in the long term, but also helps weaken an extortion model that systematically harms CSOs.

6. Seek support and document what happened.

   You do not have to face a ransomware attack alone. We understand many CSOs and grassroots organizations operate with limited resources and may not always be able to access external assistance. When possible, reach out to trusted technical staff, peer organizations, civil society networks, or pro bono experts. It is also important to notify relevant authorities or law enforcement, who can provide guidance and help track the attack. Their support can make a real difference in managing the situation and reducing its impact.

   At the same time, carefully documenting what happened, the decisions made, and the challenges faced is crucial. Think of it as creating a roadmap for the future: this record helps your organization learn from the incident, improve practices, and prepare for any attacks ahead. Over time, sharing experiences within trusted networks can also strengthen resilience across civil society as a whole.

ATTACK PROFILE: Ransomware

Understanding the Issue: How to Spot a Ransomware Attack

- Signs of initial access, such as phishing attempts
- Signs of system compromise
- Unusual attempts to access multiple systems
- Misuse of administration tools
- Disabled defenses
- Data being sent outside the organization

Taking Action: Best Practices

- Keep software up to date.
- Use multi-factor authentication (MFA).
- Use strong passwords.
- Restrict user privileges and maintain good account hygiene.
- Use email filtering tools.
- Be aware of unverified links and attachments.
- Protect devices, not just networks.
- Make frequent backups.
- Use a VPN when connecting to public networks.
- Use a firewall, proxy, or intrusion detection system (IDS/IPS).
- Periodically review weak points.
- Adopt a "zero trust" mindset.
- Promote a culture of caution.

Learning from It: How to Respond to a Ransomware Attack

- Disconnect the device from the network and any shared connections to stop the spread.
- Note ransom messages, file changes, or instructions for technical staff to analyze.
- Clean the device with expert help after isolation and identification.
- Use secure backups to restore files and resume activities.
- Do not pay the ransom.
- Get help, record all actions, and share lessons to strengthen resilience.

Report an incident: `https://incident.protect.ngo`

Useful resources:

The IST blueprint for ransomware defense: `https://securityandtechnology.org/virtual-library/report/blueprint-for-ransomware-defense`

Spyware: Intimidation as Censorship

What Is It?

Spyware is a form of highly intrusive surveillance software designed to secretly monitor a device and extract information from it. In this chapter, spyware refers specifically to what is often described as commercial or mercenary spyware: tools developed and sold by private companies as part of commercial cyber intrusion capabilities, and primarily marketed to law enforcement or intelligence authorities.

These tools are designed to provide deep access to devices such as mobile phones or computers, allowing operators to retrieve messages (including from encrypted applications), emails, contacts, location data, and in some cases to activate microphones or cameras. Spyware differs from more common forms of malware in both its objectives and its level of sophistication. It is usually tailored for targeted surveillance rather than mass infection.

Although vendors commonly justify these technologies as being necessary for legitimate law enforcement or national security purposes, extensive investigations by civil society and technical research groups have documented patterns of abuse. Cases involving tools such as Pegasus and Predator have shown repeated use against journalists, human rights defenders, activists, and political opponents, rather than being limited to investigations of serious crime.

The most advanced spyware does not rely primarily on user error. While phishing and malicious links can still play a role in some attacks, many commercial spyware tools rely on sophisticated exploitation techniques, including so-called "zero-click" attacks that require no interaction from the target. As a result, individuals can be successfully targeted even when they follow good digital hygiene practices.

When spyware is used outside legal frameworks, or without necessity, proportionality, and independent oversight, it constitutes a serious violation of human rights, particularly the rights to privacy, freedom of expression, and freedom of association. In many documented cases, the responsibility for such violations lies with state authorities or with private actors acting on their behalf.

What Is the Danger to Civil Society?

CSOs and civil society actors, including NGOs, journalists, humanitarian organizations, lawyers, and community groups, are increasingly targeted by spyware for a wide range of reasons. While organizations documenting human rights abuses are highly exposed, they are far from the only ones at risk. Many CSOs become targets because of where they operate, the populations they support, or the political and military context in which they work.

In conflict and post-conflict settings, CSOs providing humanitarian assistance, supporting displaced populations, or working with communities affected by violence are often perceived as strategically sensitive. For example, organizations operating in or around Ukraine since the beginning of the full-scale invasion have faced surveillance because of their proximity to military activity, international funding, government actors, or vulnerable civilian populations. In such contexts, spyware can be used to monitor logistical operations, map networks of partners, or gain insight into donor coordination and cross-border support efforts.

The targeting of civil society through spyware is therefore not limited to what organizations publicly report or advocate for. It often reflects broader political, security, or geopolitical interests, where civil society infrastructure itself is seen as something to be monitored, controlled, or neutralized. Beyond information gathering, spyware is frequently used to intimidate and disrupt organizations, signaling that their activities and relationships are visible and potentially punishable.

Spyware undermines the collective nature of civil society work. By exposing internal communications, contacts, and strategies, it creates fear and uncertainty within organizations and between partners. This weakens coordination, discourages participation, and erodes trust, which are essential for effective collective action.

When CSOs operate under the assumption that their communications are monitored, they often restrict digital exchanges, reduce outreach, or avoid sensitive discussions altogether. This self-limitation can isolate organizations from international partners, donors, and support networks that could otherwise provide protection or assistance. Over time, this isolation contributes to the marginalization of civil society voices and limits their ability to influence public debate or policy.

Such surveillance rarely occurs in isolation. Investigations over the past decade have consistently shown that spyware is used as part of broader strategies aimed at weakening CSOs, independent media, and democratic opposition. These practices have been documented across a wide range of political systems and conflict contexts, and they frequently target organizations as collective entities, not only the individuals working within them.

In Mexico, for example, investigations revealed the use of spyware against journalists, anti-corruption advocates, and public health organizations, including civil society groups advocating for transparency during the so-called "war on drugs." These operations did not compromise individual phones, but affected organizational communications, internal coordination, and the protection of sources linked to CSO investigations. In a context marked by violence and impunity, this surveillance increased risks for entire organizations and their networks.

In the Middle East and North Africa, spyware has been used repeatedly against CSOs working on human rights, labor rights, and political reform in the aftermath of the Arab uprisings. Investigations have documented surveillance against CSOs and their staff in Jordan, where a multi-year operation uncovered in 2024 showed spyware being used against dozens of civil society actors, including members of associations and staff linked to international nonprofits. The surveillance occurred alongside legal pressure, online harassment, and restrictions on civic activity, directly affecting organizational capacity and staff well-being.

Cross-border repression has also impacted CSOs operating in exile or supporting opposition movements abroad. Spyware has been used against diaspora organizations, independent media outlets, and CSOs documenting abuses by authoritarian governments. In cases linked to Saudi Arabia, digital surveillance targeted not only individual dissidents but also organizations, journalists' networks, and human rights groups connected to the work of Jamal Khashoggi, demonstrating how organizations' ecosystems can be mapped and disrupted across borders.

Europe has seen similar patterns. Citizen Lab, Access Now, and Amnesty International have documented spyware use against journalists and CSOs in EU member states including Poland, Hungary, and Greece. In these cases, surveillance affected newsrooms as well as various CSOs, including watchdog organizations and advocacy groups investigating government conduct. Spyware use coincided with political crises, electoral competition, and efforts to control media narratives, showing that organizational targeting can occur even within formal democratic systems when safeguards are weakened.

In conflict-affected and high-tension contexts, spyware has been used against humanitarian organizations, civil society groups, and CSOs reporting on military operations, war crimes, or human rights violations. Surveillance in these settings places organizations at heightened risk, as compromised communications can expose staff movements, beneficiaries, sources, and sensitive operational information. The consequences extend beyond the organization itself, potentially endangering civilians and partners connected to its work.

Across these contexts, spyware is frequently combined with other repressive measures targeting organizations directly: arrests and detention of staff members, judicial harassment of CSOs through abusive laws, restrictions on funding and registration, and coordinated online smear campaigns. Together, these practices contribute to self-censorship, organizational fatigue, and burnout, progressively shrinking civic space. In this environment, surveillance becomes not an isolated abuse, but one component of a wider system designed to disrupt civil society and limit democratic participation.

What About Society as a Whole?

The use of spyware represents a serious threat to society beyond the individuals or organizations directly targeted. By enabling covert surveillance, it allows state authorities and other actors to monitor citizens, public officials, and civil society actors both within and beyond national borders. This has implications not only for those living in a given country, but also for diasporas, exile communities, and transnational networks that rely on cross-border communication to operate safely.

Spyware is not inherently deployed with the explicit aim of causing physical harm. However, when abused, it can lead to extremely severe consequences. Investigations have shown that covert surveillance has been used to locate individuals, expose their networks, or identify moments of vulnerability, creating conditions that precede arrests, enforced disappearance, violent reprisals, or other forms of repression (Figure 2.7). Even in the absence of physical violence, sustained surveillance and the harassment that often accompanies it have profound psychological effects, including fear, anxiety, loss of trust, and long-term trauma for those affected and their communities.

More broadly, democratic systems themselves are weakened when espionage becomes a tool of political control rather than a strictly regulated and exceptional measure. Journalists, activists, lawyers, and whistleblowers play a critical role in informing the public, exposing wrongdoing, and holding power to account. When they are subjected to digital intimidation, prevented from speaking freely, or pushed into self-censorship for their own safety, the impact extends to society as a whole. Freedoms of expression and association, media independence, and the right to protest are all undermined when surveillance is normalized or left unchecked.

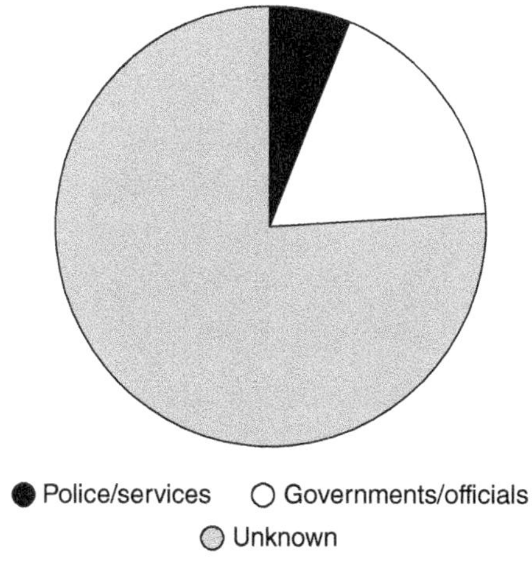

FIGURE 2.7 Spyware uses in Europe, 2020–2025.

Source: Adapted from European Centre for Press and Media Freedom (ECPMF) (2025)

States continue to struggle with the legal and political challenge of regulating spyware effectively. While recent years have seen increased international discussion, including at the European level through initiatives such as the Pall Mall Process launched with the involvement of France and the United Kingdom, these efforts remain limited in scope and largely nonbinding. One of the main obstacles to accountability is attribution. Spyware operations are intentionally designed to obscure responsibility, and in a significant proportion of documented cases it is not possible to clearly identify the operator or the authority behind the surveillance.

Large-scale investigations have nonetheless provided insight into the scope of the problem. In 2020, the Pegasus Project, a collaboration between CSOs and investigative media, revealed the global spread of commercial spyware and its repeated use against journalists, activists, and political actors across dozens of countries. While the project did not establish confirmed infections for every case identified, it demonstrated how such tools had migrated far beyond their stated purpose of combating serious crime or terrorism and into routine political surveillance.

The private sector plays a central role in this ecosystem. Spyware is developed, sold, and maintained by commercial vendors operating across jurisdictions and regulatory gaps. Repeated investigations by civil society have shown that existing safeguards are insufficient to prevent misuse. Voluntary initiatives and diplomatic processes have so far failed to establish effective accountability, and in some cases have raised concerns about reputational laundering, where companies implicated in abuse seek legitimacy through participation in policy discussions. Without binding rules, transparent oversight, and meaningful enforcement, the risks posed by spyware to individuals, civil society, and democratic society as a whole are likely to persist and deepen.

Understanding the Issue: How to Recognize Warning Signs

Spyware rarely announces itself. It does not usually cause dramatic crashes or clear warning messages. The most advanced forms are designed to operate silently, blending into normal device behavior and taking advantage of the fact that people are busy, overstretched, and working under pressure. In many cases, a device can be compromised without the user noticing any obvious sign at all.

Recognizing a potential spyware incident is therefore less about identifying a single technical indicator and more about noticing patterns that feel out of place. Changes that cannot be explained by a software update, a new application, or heavier-than-usual use deserve attention. Devices may become slower or less responsive, overheat during light use, or experience unusually fast battery drain. On their own, these symptoms are common and often harmless, but when several appear together, especially in a high-risk context, they should not be dismissed.

Unexpected pop-up ads, unfamiliar messages, or unexplained changes to browser settings, such as a new homepage or search engine, can also indicate that unwanted software is running in the background. These signs are more typical of lower-level spyware or other forms of malware, but they still warrant caution, particularly if they appear alongside other concerns.

1. Difficulty accessing trusted devices.

   Repeated problems logging into familiar accounts can be an important warning sign. If access fails intermittently, or if accounts behave differently without a clear reason, it may indicate interference. This is especially concerning when it affects email accounts, shared work platforms, financial systems, or donor databases, where compromise can have consequences for an entire organization rather than a single individual. However, connection issues and security controls can also generate similar symptoms, so these signals should be considered as part of a broader picture, not as confirmation on their own.

2. Unexplained increases in data usage.

   Some forms of spyware transmit collected information to external servers. In certain cases, this may result in sustained or unexplained increases in data or bandwidth usage. While this is not a reliable indicator of advanced spyware, it can add to a broader set of warning signs and justify closer examination, particularly for devices handling sensitive information.

3. Unusual device activity.

   More unsettling signs can also occur. Camera or microphone indicators activating without a clear reason, unexpected system notifications, or interference during calls may point to suspicious activity. These indicators do not automatically mean that spyware is present, but they should be taken seriously when combined with other unusual behavior or when the individual or organization is operating in a sensitive environment.

4. Signs that your device has been unlocked without your knowledge.

   Some spyware relies on bypassing a device's built-in protections. On iPhones, this can involve *jailbreaking*, which removes Apple's security restrictions and allows software to be installed outside the App Store. On Android devices, *rooting* grants full administrator access and allows applications to control or remove other apps.

   Unless these changes were made deliberately and for a specific, well-understood purpose, a jailbroken or rooted device represents a significantly higher risk and should be treated with caution. In many professional and organizational contexts, such modifications are incompatible with basic security expectations.

5. Unfamiliar programs running on your computer.

   Spyware can also affect laptops and desktop computers. On Windows or macOS, malicious software can run quietly in the background without drawing attention. Noticing an unfamiliar program or process does not automatically mean there is a problem, as operating systems run many background services. However, if a program cannot be explained or linked to legitimate work, it should not be ignored. Pausing activity and informing an internal IT contact, a digital security focal point, or a supervisor allows the organization to assess the situation before further action is taken.

Taking Action: Best Practices

1. Keep systems up to date.

   Regular software and operating system updates are one of the most effective basic protections available. Updates repair known vulnerabilities that spyware developers actively exploit. While updates can be inconvenient during busy periods, postponing them increases exposure, particularly for phones and laptops used for sensitive civil society work.

2. Strengthen baseline protection.

   Reputable antivirus and anti-malware tools help defend against common threats and can alert users to suspicious activity. They are not designed to reliably detect the most advanced commercial spyware, and should not be relied on as a guarantee of safety. However, they still provide value by reducing exposure to simpler attacks and should be installed and kept active on all organizational devices.

3. Limit administrator privileges.

   Daily work should be done without administrator or "root" access whenever possible. Accounts with elevated permissions make it easier for spyware to embed itself deeply into a system. Using standard user accounts for routine tasks helps contain potential damage if a device is compromised.

4. Avoid risky device modifications.

   Rooting Android devices or *jailbreaking* iPhones removes critical security protections and significantly increases vulnerability to spyware and other surveillance tools. Unless there is a clear, operational need and the risks are fully understood and managed, these practices should be avoided in civil society contexts.

5. Enable Lockdown Mode on Apple devices.

   Apple's Lockdown Mode is designed for people who may be deliberately targeted because of their work or public role. It reduces the number of features and connections available to minimize attack surfaces. While it limits some functions, it can provide meaningful additional protection for high-risk individuals and organizations when used deliberately and with informed consent.

6. Protect everyday connections.

   Public or unsecured Wi-Fi networks can expose devices to interception or manipulation. This risk increases during travel, public events, or remote work. When such networks cannot be avoided, using a trusted VPN can reduce exposure, though it does not eliminate all risks.

7. Be intentional about app permissions.

   Applications requesting access to cameras, microphones, contacts, or files should have a clear and legitimate reason for doing so. Permissions that do not align with an app's function are a warning sign. Regularly reviewing permissions and removing unnecessary applications help limit opportunities for silent surveillance.

8. Restart devices regularly.

   Some malicious processes operate only in temporary memory. Restarting devices can interrupt certain forms of low-level or short-lived attacks. This is not a defense against advanced spyware, but it can still disrupt some threats with minimal effort.

9. Use secure and privacy-enhancing tools.

   Encrypted communication, secure file storage, strong passwords managed through a password manager, and multi-factor authentication (MFA) all reduce the broader impact of a compromised device. These measures are particularly important for shared accounts and organizational platforms, where a single breach can cascade across teams.

10. Build internal awareness and support.

    Spyware prevention and response are organizational responsibilities. Staff should feel able to report concerns without fear of blame. Regular discussions, clear guidance, and designated points of contact support early detection and coordinated responses.

11. Monitor and document.

    Keeping simple, secure records of unusual behavior, suspected incidents, and actions taken creates an internal memory that supports learning and accountability. Documentation can later enable technical analysis, legal action, or engagement with trusted external support. When investigation feels overwhelming or risky, starting with careful observation and seeking advice early can prevent harm.

Suspicion of Spyware: Immediate Response Checklist

This checklist is designed for situations where spyware is suspected, not confirmed. It prioritizes safety, evidence preservation, and organizational response, not technical certainty.

1. Slow down and do not act alone.
   - Do **not** panic and do not try to “fix” the problem immediately.
   - Do **not** delete apps, reset devices, or run unfamiliar tools as a first reaction.
   - Treat the situation as an organizational issue, not a personal mistake.

The first objective is to avoid making the situation worse or destroying potential evidence.

2. Assess the immediate risk.

   Ask yourself (or the organization’s focal point):

   - Is the device used for sensitive work (human rights, humanitarian action, journalism, legal support, conflict-related activity)?
   - Could the compromise affect other people (colleagues, partners, beneficiaries, sources)?
   - Is there a current threat context (harassment, arrests, legal pressure, conflict escalation)?

If the answer to any of these is yes, treat the situation as high-risk.

3. Limit exposure (containment).
   - Disconnect the device from networks:
     - Turn off Wi-Fi, mobile data, and Bluetooth.

  - If possible, remove the SIM card.
- Avoid logging into sensitive accounts from the suspected device.
- Do not move files from the device to other work systems.

This helps reduce ongoing data exfiltration and prevents wider compromise.

4. Preserve information and context.

   Before any technical intervention:

   - Note what raised concern (unusual behavior, alerts, messages, context).
   - Record dates, times, and circumstances (travel, meetings, incidents, campaigns).
   - Take screenshots or photos of unusual messages, settings, or notifications.

Keep this information secure and share it only with trusted people.

5. Inform internally.

   - Notify your organization's IT contact, digital security focal point, or management.
   - If none exists, make sure at least one trusted person is aware.
   - Avoid discussing the issue on potentially compromised communication channels.

   Clear internal awareness helps coordinated decision-making.

6. Seek trusted external support early.

   Do not investigate complex spyware incidents alone. You can always contact Protect-ngo and, should we not be able to help you, we will make sure you find help. The bottom line: do not investigate complex spyware incidents alone. Depending on your context, you may seek support from:

- **Access Now—Digital Security Helpline**

  Provides confidential support to CSOs, journalists, and human rights defenders at risk, including guidance after suspected spyware targeting and coordination with trusted technical partners.
- **Amnesty International Security Lab (Amnesty Tech)**

  Offers forensic support in selected cases and publishes tools and methodologies used to detect and analyze spyware targeting civil society. Access is prioritized for high-risk human rights cases.
- **Citizen Lab (University of Toronto)**

  Conducts in-depth technical investigations into advanced spyware campaigns. Citizen Lab does not provide a general helpline but may engage in cases with strong public interest, documented patterns, or strategic relevance.
- **Trusted regional or thematic digital security organizations**

  In some contexts, local or regional civil society technology organizations may be the safest first point of contact and can help assess whether escalation is appropriate.

These organizations can help assess risk, advise on next steps, and determine whether forensic analysis, legal action, or advocacy is appropriate.

7. Avoid common mistakes.

   Until you receive expert advice:

- Do not factory-reset the device "just in case."
- Do not uninstall suspicious apps in high-risk cases.

- Do not attempt advanced technical analysis without guidance.
- Do not assume the problem is solved because symptoms disappear.

Many advanced spyware tools are designed to survive or evade quick fixes.

8. Protect people, not just devices.
   - Check in with affected staff: fear, guilt, or anxiety are common.
   - Reaffirm that being targeted is not a failure or negligence.
   - Allow time to recover and adjust work expectations if needed.

   Psychological safety is part of digital safety.

9. Review organizational impact.

   Once the immediate risk is stabilized, consider the following:

   - Which communications or projects may have been exposed
   - Whether partners, beneficiaries, or sources could be affected
   - Whether legal, donor, or duty-of-care obligations apply

   This step helps limit secondary harm.

10. Learn and strengthen.

    After the incident (or suspected incident):

    - Document lessons learned.
    - Adjust internal practices or access controls if needed.
    - Identify a clear contact point and process for future incidents.

    Preparedness reduces panic and harm next time.

Key reminder:

- You do not need proof of infection to take concerns seriously.
- Early caution, collective response, and trusted support are always safer than certainty sought alone.

ATTACK PROFILE: Spyware (Quick Response)

Understanding the Issue: How to Recognize Warning Signs

Spyware is designed to stay hidden. There may be no single clear signal. Pay attention when several warning signs appear together, especially in sensitive or high-risk contexts. Watch for:

- Difficulty accessing trusted accounts or devices
- Unexplained increases in data or bandwidth usage
- Unusual device behavior (battery drain, overheating, camera or microphone indicators activating unexpectedly)
- Signs a device has been jailbroken or rooted without intent
- Unfamiliar programs or processes on computers

Taking Action: Best Practices

- Keep operating systems and apps up to date.
- Use reputable antivirus or anti-malware tools (with realistic expectations).
- Avoid administrator or "root" access for daily work.
- Do not jailbreak or root devices unless strictly necessary.

- Enable Lockdown Mode on Apple devices for high-risk staff.
- Be cautious on public Wi-Fi; use trusted VPNs when needed.
- Review app permissions regularly.
- Restart your devices regularly (helps disrupt some low-level threats).
- Use password managers and MFA.
- Be cautious with pop-ups, prompts, and downloads.
- Encourage early reporting of concerns, without blame.
- Monitor and document unusual behavior.

Learning from It: How to Respond if Spyware Is Suspected

- Slow down; do not panic or attempt quick fixes.
- Disconnect affected devices from the Internet and avoid sensitive logins.
- Preserve evidence and document what raised concern (dates, context, screenshots).
- Get help early by contacting IT or trusted external support (see the following list).
- Clean carefully (with advice)—avoid resets or app removal unless recommended.
- Secure accounts by updating passwords and strengthening protections where needed.
- Support people: treat this as an organizational issue, not an individual failure.

(*continued*)

(*continued*)

Report an incident: https://incident.protect.ngo

Useful resources:

- Access Now—Digital Security Helpline: https://www.accessnow.org/help
- Amnesty International Tech & Security Lab: https://www.amnesty.org/en/tech
- Citizen Lab (Targeted Surveillance): https://citizenlab.ca/focus-area/targeted-surveillance

CEO Fraud: The Impersonation Technique

What Is It?

CEO fraud refers to the act of assuming the identity of the CEO or of a high-ranking employee within the CSO in order to deceive one or multiple staff members for financial gain. It can also work in reverse: a decision-maker within the organization is abused through targeted fakes and misled into sending valuable assets to criminal groups. This can happen via any communication means. It can be done through email (this is called *business email compromise*), text, or, more and more frequently, via phone or even video call. The latter is achieved with the help of deepfakes—sounds, pictures, or videos generated by AI. At the end of this chapter, I will come back to the malicious use of AI tools, but it's important to understand that this technology is developing at an impressive pace and is now able to fool victims easily. By assuming the identity of the CEO or of an employee, the attackers exploit this position of power or the trust within the organization's staff to issue orders. Most often, they demand the transfer of a large sum of money, supposedly to support the CSO's mission. They then intercept this money for their own gain.

This type of attack falls under the scope of *spear phishing*. Spear phishing is defined as a phishing attack that isn't part of a wide campaign but instead targets an individual or an entity specifically. In these cases, we generally notice a large amount of details known by the attacker, who uses them in order to manipulate their victim in the most efficient way possible. While phishing campaigns target a broad audience, hoping that some targets will fall into the trap, spear phishing attacks focus on a single victim but are prepared with far greater precision. Criminals thus maximize their chances of success, and the consequences can be devastating.

What Is the Danger to Civil Society?

When we work for a nonprofit, wire transfers are common, and it wouldn't be surprising for the CEO themselves to request that one be made. The urgency of the work CSOs do is taken advantage of during these attacks: criminals pressure the targeted employee by drowning them in messages or phone calls demanding that the money be transferred rapidly. Therefore, the employee might not take the time to ask themselves whether the request is unusual or to contact the person requesting the wire through a different communication channel to ensure the message is legitimate and the wire transfer is justified.

In 2020, the CEO of a CSO operating in a war zone was on a work trip when he received a message from his financial team asking him to approve the transfer of USD 500,000. The message mentioned details related to the CEO's trips, the people he was traveling with, and the country to which the money would be sent. Since all the details were accurate and the money was to be sent to a geographical area in which the organization operated, the CEO gave his approval. Only upon his return did he realize he had been the victim of a fraudulent attack. Posing as his employees and taking advantage of his trust, the cybercriminals had sent his permission to his bank, which had wired the requested sum to a bank in China. Other attacks had also followed. Unfortunately, when the CEO realized it had been an attack, the money had already been withdrawn. Despite the collaboration of the technical teams as well as the FBI, the money was not found. For this CSO, the loss amounted to USD 1.34 million, and the CEO was forced to take out a personal loan in order to pay his employees and continue his mission.

What About Society as a Whole?

CEO fraud can target any entity, whether it's an organization or a private company. Since the motive for this type of attack is financial, cybercriminals follow the money and pick the targets that seem the most profitable. In 2024, the FBI estimated CEO fraud led to the loss of USD 2.7 billion for American businesses alone. In fact, civil society is far from being the only victim of CEO fraud attacks, and it may even seem much more profitable to target private sector companies. But let's not forget the substantial sums of money that CSOs handle each year through the donations they receive, nor their reputation as easy targets. Let's also not forget that most CSOs are very open about their wealth, as they have to publicly thank donors or publish detailed financial statements. In many cases, CSOs' compliance with financial oversight creates opportunities for criminals. We must also keep in mind the consequences: when an organization appears to be a prime target and the attack succeeds, it's not just financial losses for a multinational corporation or a drop in stock market value—it's human lives and fundamental rights that are directly impacted. The stakes in protecting nonprofits against fraud are extremely high.

Understanding the Issue: How to Spot CEO Fraud Attempts

CEO fraud rarely looks like an obvious scam. The most effective attempts often appear routine, authoritative, and urgent. Spotting them is less about technical expertise and more about developing the habit of slowing down, especially when juggling multiple roles, deadlines, or donor requests.

Many of the warning signs overlap with phishing attacks. This is not a coincidence. CEO fraud relies on the same pressures, urgency, authority, and secrecy, but adapts them to the internal life of an organization.

1. Urgency and authority are the biggest red flags.

   CEO fraud messages almost always try to rush you, often while invoking senior authority. The request may come from the executive director, a board member, or a senior manager, often someone whose time is scarce and whose instructions are rarely questioned.

   You may be told that a payment must be made immediately, that a sensitive issue requires discretion, or that delays could have serious consequences. This urgency is intentional. It is designed to override normal judgment and procedures.

When a request pressures you to act quickly and quietly, pause. Legitimate leaders expect verification, even in fast-moving situations, and understand that confirming a request protects both staff and the organization.

2. Requests that break routine deserve extra attention.

   CEO fraud often involves requests that fall outside everyday practice. These may include asking for an exceptional payment, bypassing approvals, sharing sensitive information by email, or handling a matter "just this once" outside standard channels.

   Pay attention when a request asks you to do something you would normally double-check, escalate, or document. Even in small organizations where roles overlap, unusual requests should slow things down, not speed them up.

3. The sender may feel familiar, but something is off.

   Many CEO fraud attempts impersonate people you know. The name may be correct, the role familiar, and the tone authoritative. This familiarity is part of the manipulation, especially in organizations built on trust, long-standing relationships, and informal communication.

   However, small changes in spelling, public email domains, or addresses that closely resemble official ones are common. Also notice changes in writing style, tone, or level of formality. Messages that feel oddly polished, unusually brief, or strangely generic are worth questioning. One detail alone may not mean much, but patterns matter.

4. Voice and video requests (deepfakes).

   CEO fraud is no longer limited to email. Attackers increasingly use voice messages or video calls that imitate senior leaders. These may sound convincing, but they should not be treated as proof of legitimacy. Technical issues that limit interaction, prevent questions, or force one-way communication can be part of the tactic, particularly when teams lack dedicated IT support to troubleshoot in real time.

Taking Action: Best Practices

CEO fraud is the second most common type of attack deployed against CSOs, and because it falls under social engineering, the good practices mentioned for cases of phishing at the start of this chapter are also applicable here. In addition to these, other practices can be put in place.

1. Make verification normal, not exceptional.

   Any request involving payments, transfers, or sensitive information should be verified through a different communication channel (for example, a phone or video call). This means using contact details you already trust, not those provided in the message itself.

   Verification is not a sign of distrust. It is a routine safeguard that protects staff as much as the organization. In smaller teams, this may be as simple as checking with a colleague or supervisor before acting.

2. Keep financial controls simple and clear.

   CEO fraud thrives when one person is pressured to act alone. Nonprofits can reduce this risk by applying clear internal payment protocols and consistently following financial and procurement policies. Simple controls, such as verifying the legitimacy of payment requests received by email and requiring a second person to review or approve unusual bank transfers, grant disbursements, or payments above an established threshold, can be highly effective. These measures do not need to be complex or bureaucratic; what matters is that no one feels compelled to make high-stakes decisions in isolation.

3. Share less information online than attackers expect.

   Public information about staff roles, internal processes, or leadership routines can be used to craft convincing impersonation attempts. Periodically review what your organization shares online and in open forums.

   Help staff understand how small details (job titles, reporting lines, travel plans) can be misused. Reducing exposure makes targeted attacks harder. Clearly defined and well-communicated policies help protect staff and the organization from social engineering attacks. When people understand what information to share, they are better equipped to reduce risks for themselves and the organization.

4. Train everyone, regularly.

   CEO fraud does not target only finance teams. Awareness should extend to all staff, including leadership (in the example cited earlier, it was the head of the organization himself who was targeted). Practical, regular training, especially for new employees, is essential to help teams stay on the lookout for scams. Taking note of real-world examples will help everyone in the organization recognize the red flags.

   Reinforce one simple message: if something feels urgent, secret, or unusual, slowing down is the right response.

   - Use technical protections as support.
   - Basic technical measures such as email filtering, strong passwords, and MFA reduce risk and ease pressure on staff. Where possible, configuring email authentication protocols such as DMARC, DKIM, or SPF can also reduce the chances of email spoofing. These tools do not replace judgment, but they give teams more space to make careful

decisions, especially when time, staff, or technical capacity are limited.

- Put in place an incident response plan.

Every CSO should have clear guidance on what to do if staff notice a suspicious email or request. Acting quickly and reporting concerns right away can help reduce damage and protect funds and information.

5. Foster a culture of transparency.

Promoting a culture of transparency means encouraging open communication and information sharing within the organization. When staff feel confident asking questions, verifying unusual requests, and reporting concerns without fear of retaliation, the risk is significantly reduced.

Learning from It: What to Do After a CEO Fraud Attack

First of all, it's important to remind everyone that CEO fraud is not the result of personal failure. Well-designed attacks exploit trust, authority, and time pressure. What matters most is how quickly and calmly the organization responds. In the first moments after a suspected incident, the goal is not to assign blame or fully understand what happened. The priority is to limit harm and preserve information.

1. Act quickly to limit the damage.

If money may have been transferred, contact your bank immediately and ask whether the transaction can be stopped or reversed. If another bank is involved, request that funds be frozen if possible. Document what happened and when.

2. Alert others and follow internal steps.

Inform leadership and relevant colleagues as soon as possible. Early awareness can prevent further harm, especially if the same tactic is used elsewhere in the organization. If internal response steps exist, follow them. If they do not, this incident highlights the value of defining a few clear actions for the future.

3. Preserve information and report the incident.

   Save all related emails, messages, call records, and payment confirmations. Do not delete or modify them.

   Report the incident to relevant authorities, even if losses were avoided. Reporting helps protect other organizations and contributes to broader understanding of attack patterns.

4. Turn the incident into learning.

   Once the immediate risk has passed, take time to reflect. What made the request convincing? Where did uncertainty arise? Sharing these lessons openly, within the organization or with trusted peer networks, strengthens collective awareness and reduces the likelihood of similar incidents in the future.

ATTACK PROFILE: CEO Fraud

Understanding the Issue: How to Spot CEO Fraud Attempts

- Urgency and secrecy
- Unusual requests
- Small changes in spelling, public email domains, or addresses that closely resemble official ones
- Voice and video requests

Taking Action: Best Practices

- Always verify payment or data requests.
- Use a second channel to confirm.
- Involve more than one person in decisions.
- Limit publicly available internal information.
- Establish internal protocols and policies.
- Train staff to recognize red flags.
- Use technical protections: MFA, email authentication protocols (DMARC, DKIM, SPF), email filtering, strong passwords.
- Foster a culture of transparency.

Learning from It: What to Do After a CEO Fraud Attack

- Act quickly if something goes wrong.
- Alert others and follow internal steps.
- Preserve all evidence.
- Contact banks immediately.
- Report the incident.
- Turn the incident into learning.

Report an incident: `https://incident.protect.ngo`

Information Manipulation: Eroding Trust and Undermining Missions

For many, a criminal act or a human rights violation leveraging information manipulation does not constitute a cyberattack. I would push back on this. For malicious state actors and criminal groups, information manipulation, with all its variations—disinformation, foreign interference—is one of the many cyber-attack vectors at their disposal. More importantly, for CSOs, it is just one of the many digital threats they face and is nowadays a critical component of hybrid operations conducted by adversaries.

What Is It?

Information manipulation is defined as a behavioral pattern that threatens or can potentially negatively impact political values and processes. It is characterized by a conscious and coordinated will to manipulate. The objective is for the person who receives the information to interpret it wrongly or be misled by it. Information manipulation is used by state and nonstate actors alike and can refer to various types of content and behavior: bots, propaganda, trolls, and many more.

When it comes to this practice, there is always an intention of interfering with the way the information is received or interpreted. This can be done through various means: first, distortion, which includes, for example, amplification and suppression. These tactics consist of exaggerating the information, emphasizing certain aspects of it, or isolating it from its context, thus hiding additional information which could potentially influence the way the receiver interprets the message. Censorship, for example, falls under the distortion tactic category. Information manipulation also includes the behavior of users: the speed at which the information is shared, who shares it or interacts with it, and how. Another tactic, called *disinformation*, is defined as the propagation of information which is simply false or misleading, in an intentional manner. It has existed in cyberspace for a while, but a new type of disinformation has emerged in recent years: deepfakes. I've already mentioned them regarding CEO fraud: this AI-generated content replicates the voice or appearance of a person in order to lead the public to believe they said or did certain things. Deepfakes can have a comical or pornographic use, but can also be political. They are a type of disinformation using visual mediums and/or sounds.

A note on the word "disinformation": it tends to be used in everyday speech to include all these tactics, but when speaking broadly, it's more accurate to use the expression "information manipulation." Here's why: nowadays, most people get their information from sources such as television or social media. The all-encompassing notion of information manipulation includes mechanisms such as broadcasting, contextualization, and visibility rate. Today, the impact of a message largely depends on its circulation. It's not enough for the information to be accurate; it has to be circulated in such a way that its interpretation by the public reflects reality.

Information manipulation has a strong practical impact but is also symbolic. It causes harm to the fundamental rights that uphold democracy and the rule of law. It gets in the way of our ability to access reliable information and to express ourselves freely.

What Is the Danger to Civil Society?

Information manipulation campaigns can impact civil society in one of two ways: directly and, most often, indirectly. In the latter, they generally target subjects that organizations defend rather than the organizations themselves. For example, information manipulation can impact subjects linked to LGBTQ+ rights without directly attacking the organizations defending them, but by speaking more broadly about "woke culture" or "moral decadence." Similarly, a campaign can target institutions such as the United Nations or, more recently, USAID. Although these are not part of civil society themselves, many CSOs depend on them and can be strongly impacted.

However, CSOs are sometimes targeted by information manipulation campaigns in a more direct way, especially if they have high visibility. In these cases, the campaigns aim to spread false or misleading information about the organizations themselves (the work they do, the way they operate, their core missions or beliefs) rather than the subjects or communities they defend. CSOs can be used as a stake within information wars and be attacked as part of a strategy to control the narrative of a situation or conflict.

In 2024, Chinese actors coordinated an influence operation as part of an extended online information manipulation operation that has been targeting foreign dissidents and journalists since 2017. Following the deadly floods that struck the city and surroundings of Valencia, Spain, in late October, the attackers disguised themselves as a human rights organization based in Spain. Under this false identity, they took to social media and spread calls to overturn the Spanish government under the pretense that it had failed to protect its citizens effectively during the floods. Dozens of accounts have been identified as being part of this campaign, condemning Prime Minister Pedro Sánchez and his government, as well as the regional administration. The campaign was centered around a video showing a masked individual denouncing the authorities for abandoning the population. The logo of the targeted nonprofit appeared in the video, which ended with a clear call to overturn the government.

This wasn't the first attack against this organization within this extended Chinese-led information manipulation campaign. The nonprofit had been targeted multiple times in 2022, when it spoke out against certain actions taken by the Chinese government. It has since been the victim of multiple campaigns aiming to discredit it and to spread doubt around its work.

As this example illustrates, information manipulation, even when it targets a CSO and not a government directly, often has geopolitical implications. We could even argue that it is inherently political, since it consists of hindering cyberspace users' access to accurate and properly contextualized information. Politics and the fight against information manipulation are often linked. Let's take, for example, the country of Georgia, where the government resorts to anti-Western and anti-democratic propaganda techniques, largely influenced by the Kremlin and relayed by traditional media. In early 2025, Meta, the company that owns social networks such as Facebook and Instagram, announced that it would take a step backward in terms of fact-checking and adopt a system of "community ratings," just like `x.com` (Twitter). A representative of the Georgian Parliament then spoke in favor of this initiative, stating that it was a "more democratic" practice. According to him, Meta's fact-checking techniques in Georgia had previously relied primarily on two CSOs whose leaders he considered biased against the state. A closer look reveals that the mission of these two nonprofits is to fight for the integrity of information in their country. One of them, in particular, whose leader was mentioned by name by the government representative, operates through fact-checking and discourse analysis. It also conducts investigations, notably related to government information manipulation, and discredits its opponents by publicly denouncing them. Following this attack by the government, the nonprofit was informed that the Anti-Corruption Bureau had launched an investigation into it. For corrupt governments, which use information manipulation as a weapon against their own population, it is essential to do everything possible to silence those who try to expose their malicious and anti-democratic practices. On this issue, as on many others, civil society is on the frontlines and finds itself particularly exposed.

What About Society as a Whole?

Launching large-scale information manipulation campaigns requires far less technical capability than carrying out other types of cyberattacks. It's a very accessible tactic, especially nowadays, with the help of AI and social media—on which false information spreads six times faster than the truth does. That's why over these past few years, we have seen a convergence between cyberattacks and information manipulation. In order to fight against it, our understanding of this practice must evolve; we must now consider it a multi-platform, multi-actor phenomenon that threatens democratic resilience. The knowledge of academics, journalists, independent researchers, and civil society actors is essential to lead the fight against information manipulation. They can help bring emerging threats to light and inform the policies of institutions such as the European Union.

In a 2023 report about foreign interference in democratic processes, the European Parliament states that reducing the amount of information manipulation online "is a matter of public interest," as these types of operations affect "the ability of citizens to take informed decisions." Regarding the health sector, the report claims that information manipulation "erodes public trust in science, public institutions, authorities and medical staff" and therefore is a grave threat to public health. It specifies that during the COVID-19 pandemic, the propagation of misleading or false information participated in promoting fake treatments and dissuaded part of the public from getting vaccinated. According to EU DisinfoLab, a European CSO fighting against information manipulation, false narratives about climate issues also take root, evolve, and circulate extremely fast in the digital sphere, hindering policy-making.

Information manipulation plays a significant geopolitical role and can constitute a genuine strategy in conflicts and inter-state relations in general. "Information warfare" is a particularly important component of the war between Russia and Ukraine—the latter, over the years and well before the official start of the war, developed a highly effective communication strategy. Given Russia's well-known history of information manipulation, the Ukrainian state has been investing heavily to improve its image in the eyes of the European Union and other countries and to counter the often misleading information disseminated by its invader. Ukraine has established a PR Army, operating as an NGO, with multiple communication objectives: to disseminate war narratives in order to elicit a favorable emotional response to Ukraine; to call for a general boycott of Russia and Russian products; to control the narrative surrounding the war; and to spread doubt regarding information shared by Russia. Ukrainian civilians are fully involved in these efforts, widely sharing images that portray heroic civilian and military resistance to the invasion. These efforts by Ukraine have been met with some success; they have notably contributed to increased military aid from the West, as well as generating broad support for economic sanctions against Russia. The PR Army now has a website and a presence on social media (Facebook and Instagram).

In terms of measures taken, the European Union has chosen to treat information manipulation as content of a problematic, but not strictly illegal, nature. In 2018, it put in place a Code of Good Practices against Disinformation, which was then strengthened in 2022. Among other things, it commits to limiting income for websites spreading false information, enhanced transparency about sponsored content, and better collaboration with fact-checkers. Since 13 February 2025, these commitments have been integrated into the Digital Services Act, an EU regulation aiming for stricter control of large digital platforms (Google, Facebook, TikTok...). They have therefore become more restrictive.

On an international level, some measures exist, but their enforcement faces multiple obstacles. Whereas the EU remains cautious in its juridical definition of information manipulation in order to avoid any challenge to freedom of speech, on a global scale this limit is reinforced by the fact that the servers of most large social media platforms are located in the United States. That country ensures a very strong protection of freedom of speech as stated in the First Amendment of its Constitution. This concept is being increasingly manipulated in public debate by influential political and economic figures, notably Donald Trump and Elon Musk. Freedom of speech allows them to justify discourse that could fall under extremism or information manipulation and to reject any type of content moderation. This drift makes it that much more difficult to fight information manipulation campaigns.

Understanding the Issue: How to Spot Information Manipulation

Information manipulation rarely presents itself as an obvious lie. It often takes the form of breaking news, a "leak," or an emotional testimony that appears credible at first glance. For CSOs and those who support them, learning to recognize certain early warning signs is key to avoiding hasty reactions or the amplification of misleading narratives.

1. Content designed to provoke, not to inform.

   A first warning sign lies in the language of the message itself. Some messages seek to capture attention at any cost. Information manipulation often relies on exaggerated or alarmist tones, with headlines meant to shock rather than explain. Words and phrases such as "urgent," "scandal," "what they don't want you to know," or "the truth the media are hiding," often accompanied by capital letters, exclamation points, or eye-catching emojis, aim to create an artificial sense of urgency.

   It is also common for these messages to present themselves as bearers of a secret or exclusive truth. Expressions like "no one is talking about this" or "here is what really happened" suggest that the reader is part of a group with privileged access to information, when in reality this is a common tactic to reduce critical thinking.

   Another frequent signal is an extreme emotional charge. Messages that provoke fear, outrage, or disgust (for example, vague alerts about threats to children, accusations of "repugnant" behavior, or calls to anger) tend to prioritize emotional reaction over verifiable facts. In practice, very strong emotion is an invitation to pause and verify.

2. Lack of clear sources and evidence-free attacks.

   Information manipulation rarely relies on solid sources. It is common to find vague references such as "someone close to the matter," "a system insider," "someone who was there," or screenshots of supposed statements with no link or context. When it is not possible to identify who said something, when it was said, and where it was originally published, the information loses credibility.

In many cases, this content focuses on discrediting public institutions (health services, electoral authorities, courts, international organizations, or the media) through insinuations or serious accusations that are not supported by evidence. In times of crisis, such messages seek to erode public trust and generate confusion.

There are also recurring narratives, especially around sensitive topics such as migration, elections, gender, public health, or armed conflict. Even if a specific message appears new, the narrative framework is often recognizable and has been used before to polarize or manipulate.

A particularly serious indicator is the use of dehumanizing or hostile language directed at individuals or groups based on their identity (religion, ethnicity, gender, nationality, sexual orientation).

3. Misleading presentation and context manipulation.

Beyond the text, the way information is presented offers important clues. A common sign is the absence of basic details: no date, author, outlet, or clear reference, making it impossible to place the information in its real context.

Screenshots are a particularly common tactic. Headlines supposedly published by well-known outlets, statements attributed to real accounts, or excerpts from documents appear as cropped images, making it difficult to verify whether they have been altered or taken out of context. For example, a fake headline designed to resemble a recognized media outlet may circulate widely even though no such article ever existed.

It is also common to use images or videos that do not correspond to the message. Real photographs, but taken in another country or at another time, are reused to illustrate different events. A typical case is showing images of a specific community to associate it with a crime committed by a single individual, generating stigmatization.

Another frequent practice is recycling old content (videos, news articles, or statements) and presenting it as current, without clarifying the original date. Visual editing can also be misleading: dramatic music, overlaid text, selective cuts, or repetition guide the viewer toward a predetermined conclusion.

4. Suspicious behavior and dissemination patterns.

How content spreads can be as revealing as the content itself. One thing to look out for is disproportionate engagement: accounts with very few followers receiving thousands of reactions, or generic comments that are repeated and appear automated.

It is also important to check who is sharing and promoting the message. Suspicious profiles often have random names, generic images or AI-generated faces, no personal posts, and activity patterns that do not seem human (posting around the clock, repeating the same message, or engaging only with certain topics).

In some cases, the content itself appears artificial or inauthentic: overly polished texts, "too perfect" images, or videos with no clear attribution that attempt to pass as real. Another clear sign is nonorganic distribution, when the same message appears simultaneously across multiple unrelated accounts or pages, without any news event to explain it.

Finally, it's important to be cautious of websites that look like well-known media outlets but use slightly different web addresses, as well as blogs that do not clearly say who is behind them.

Taking Action: Best Practices

Preventing information manipulation does not start when a crisis erupts, but long before. For CSOs and donors, it means building an internal culture based on verification, caution, and public responsibility, avoiding the risk of becoming, even unintentionally, amplifiers of false narratives.

1. Anticipate through active monitoring.

   CSOs can use monitoring tools to keep an eye on their online presence. This can act as a first line of defense: that way, they will be alerted when they are mentioned anywhere and can take action rapidly if needed. Some monitoring tools require minimal technical skills to oversee media mentions and social media comments (e.g., Google Alerts). Thanks to this, CSOs can counter and even anticipate false narratives at early stages, better understand how they are perceived publicly, respond quickly to manipulation attempts, and recognize coordinated campaigns when the same message appears in different spaces. For teams with limited resources, assigning this task to one person or a small group, with periodic reviews and clear criteria, is often sufficient.

2. Make verification a daily practice.

   Information manipulation thrives on speed. Prevention therefore requires establishing a simple routine: stop, read carefully, check, and only then decide whether to respond, share, or ignore a piece of content.

   Verification means identifying who published the information, their track record, and the interests they may represent. Reliable sources usually provide links to documents, official statements, or other evidence supporting their claims. Cross-checking information with other outlets or organizations significantly reduces the risk of falling into manipulative narratives.

A useful guideline for CSO teams is to assume that when content triggers a very strong emotional reaction, that is precisely when it most needs calm and careful verification.

3. Treat images, screenshots, and videos with special caution.

   Screenshots and visual content are especially effective at deceiving because they "look real." Before giving them credibility, it is important to ask whether the original publication can be found on the corresponding official site or profile. When this is not possible, the safest bet is not to use that material as a basis for decisions, statements, or public positions.

   For images and videos, checking whether they have been shared before or belong to a different context can prevent mistakes. This does not require advanced techniques, but rather adopting a basic rule: if the source cannot be traced, it should not be amplified.

4. Always ask who is sharing information and why.

   Not all information deserves the same level of credibility, especially when it comes from anonymous accounts or profiles with no clear identity. Before assuming something is true, it is worth asking who is sharing it, what their relationship to the issue is, and which independent sources confirm it.

   Even when content comes from trusted individuals, it may be part of chains where the original source has been lost. Establishing an internal standard that only information attributable to real and verifiable sources is considered reliable is a highly effective preventive measure.

5. Avoid amplifying fake or coordinated activity.

   Information manipulation campaigns often use accounts that look like real people but behave in unusual ways, posting constantly, repeating the same messages, or trying to start arguments. The safest approach is not to engage with these accounts, not to share their content, and not to treat them as a trustworthy source or what they post as reliable.

6. Step outside the information bubble.

   Digital platforms prioritize content that captures attention and confirms prior beliefs. This can trap teams, communities, and donors in bubbles where repetition makes false information seem true. Diversifying information sources, consulting different outlets, and avoiding forming opinions solely based on social media help maintain a more balanced perspective.

7. Read beyond the headline and mind the tone.

   Many manipulation campaigns do not rely on completely false information. Instead, they often use real facts presented in a misleading way. For this reason, it is important not to rely only on a headline, image, or short post. Taking a moment to read the full content, check where the information comes from, and look at other sources can help avoid reacting to content meant to mislead or provoke.

   Tone also matters. Some campaigns are designed to create anger, conflict, or fatigue. While discussion and debate can be healthy, responding calmly and respectfully helps prevent situations that waste time and energy and distract from the organization's main mission.

8. Strengthen collective capacity and response plans.

   Sharing information and observations with other CSOs increases collective resilience against spikes in information manipulation. For donors and grant-makers seeking to strengthen resilience across civil society, supporting training in media literacy and crisis communication plans that include information manipulation scenarios is a strategic investment that reduces long-term risks.

Teams should also be trained to recognize the cognitive biases that make false narratives "feel true" and to use techniques such as explaining common manipulation tactics before they encounter them in real-world situations.

The Golden Rule: Think Twice Before Sharing Information manipulation depends on virality, and every individual matters. A brief pause before forwarding, commenting, or posting, especially when content is incendiary, is one of the most powerful prevention tools available.

In the CSO and donor ecosystem, this caution protects not only individual organizations, but also the public trust that underpins the work of civil society. In environments where trust is constantly under attack, disciplined information practices are not only a defensive measure, but a form of civic responsibility (Figure 2.8).

Learning from It: What to Do if You've Fallen Victim

1. Decide whether a public response is necessary.

   Before reacting, take a moment to assess whether the false information truly requires a public response. Not every misleading claim deserves attention. If the content has limited reach and has only been seen by a small audience, responding publicly can sometimes amplify the narrative, ultimately doing more harm than good. In these cases, monitoring the situation while allowing the content to fade may be the safest option.

   If the information is spreading, gaining visibility, or likely to damage trust in your organization or the communities you work with, a response becomes necessary. When action is

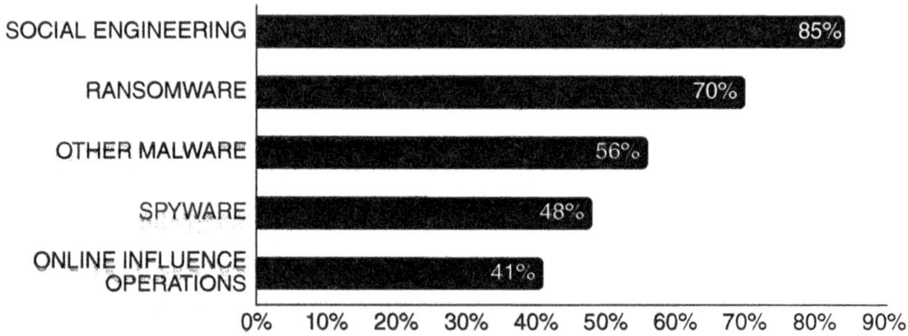

FIGURE 2.8 NGO threat perception: five most common cyberattack types.

Source: Protect·ngo, 2023

required, timing matters. The longer false narratives circulate without challenge, the harder they are to correct. Trust, once eroded, can take significant time and effort to rebuild.

2. Act quickly, but stay calm.

   Being targeted by information manipulation can be unsettling and stressful, especially when reputations, relationships, or safety are at stake. Feeling alarmed or angry is a natural reaction. Still, effective responses begin with calm decision-making.

   Silence is rarely neutral in cases of information manipulation, as these attacks thrive in gaps where accurate information is absent. Even a brief, clear response can help prevent false claims from becoming accepted as fact. This is why preparation matters. Regular monitoring of social media, messaging platforms, and public channels allows organizations to detect false narratives early and respond before they escalate.

3. Respond where the narrative is spreading.

   When you decide to respond, do so in the same spaces where the false information is circulating. This may include social media platforms, messaging apps, websites, or community forums. Meeting people where they are makes accurate information easier to find and more likely to be trusted.

Information manipulation often relies on emotionally charged language and compelling visuals. Responding with overly technical explanations or long statements can reduce impact. Clear, simple language focused on key facts is usually more effective. The aim is not to argue or persuade critics, but to make accurate information visible, accessible, and easy to share.

4. Center people and lived experience.

Human voices matter, especially in moments of uncertainty. Whenever possible, humanize your response rather than relying solely on formal statements.

Trusted partner organizations, community representatives, or respected individuals within affected communities can help communicate accurate information in ways that resonate. For smaller or under-resourced nonprofits, informal networks, peer organizations, volunteers, and supporters are often more effective and credible than official channels alone.

If it is safe to do so, leadership voices can also reinforce trust and legitimacy. Any public engagement should be carefully assessed, particularly in sensitive or high-risk environments where visibility may carry consequences.

5. Engage carefully and document thoroughly.

When it is safe and appropriate, consider reaching out directly to individuals or groups sharing false information. Providing clear evidence and requesting corrections or retractions can sometimes limit further spread. These interactions should remain factual and measured, avoiding escalation.

At the same time, document everything. Preserve screenshots, links, dates, times, and engagement patterns. This record may become critical if the situation escalates, whether for reporting to platforms, seeking legal advice, or supporting future advocacy and accountability efforts.

If false or misleading content violates platform policies, consider reporting it to the relevant service. Even though removal is not guaranteed, this can help limit reach.

6. Consider legal and institutional options with caution.

In some contexts, information manipulation that harms reputation, dignity, or safety may violate national laws. Legal or institutional channels can be an option, but they should be approached carefully.

CSOs operate in diverse political and legal environments, some of which may be hostile or unpredictable. Before involving authorities, assess potential risks, including retaliation or increased exposure. When possible, seek advice from trusted legal professionals or organizations experienced in these situations.

7. Maintain transparency and protect legitimacy.

Transparency is one of civil society's strongest sources of resilience. Organizations that consistently communicate openly, ethically, and in line with their values are better positioned to withstand false accusations.

Clear accountability practices and long-term trust with communities can make manipulated narratives less believable and information manipulation operations less effective. Over time, credibility becomes a form of protection.

8. Prepare for persistence and recovery.

Information manipulation campaigns rarely disappear quickly. Once false narratives gain momentum, countering them often requires sustained effort rather than a single response.

Keep staff, partners, and trusted networks informed. Share accurate updates, coordinate messaging, and ask for support when needed. Just as importantly, recognize the toll these situations can take on individuals and teams, and allow space for rest and recovery once the immediate pressure subsides.

Above all, do not give up. Persistence, coordination, and collective credibility are powerful tools against information manipulation. Civil society does not have to face these attacks alone, and resilience grows strongest when it is shared.

ATTACK PROFILE: Information Manipulation

Understanding the Issue: How to Spot Information Manipulation

- Provocative or urgent language designed to elicit emotion
- Missing or vague sources, unverifiable claims
- Misleading visuals or recycled content presented as new
- Abrupt or nonorganic spread patterns online

Taking Action: Best Practices

- Monitor mentions of your organization proactively.
- Develop a verification habit before sharing or reacting.
- Treat images, screenshots, and videos with heightened scrutiny.

(*continued*)

(*continued*)

- Consider who is sharing information and their possible motivations.
- Avoid engaging with clearly artificial dynamics.
- Broaden information sources to avoid echo chambers.
- Strengthen internal skills and collective response plans.

Learning from It: What to Do if You've Fallen Victim

- Respond publicly only if necessary.
- Prepare your response without panicking.
- Respond in the same spaces where the information is circulating, clearly and simply.
- Rely on the people around the organization.
- Be vigilant when interacting and document as much as possible.
- Examine the legal and institutional options at your disposal.
- Be transparent in your responses and interactions so as to protect the organization's credibility.

Report an incident: `https://incident.protect.ngo`

Weaponization of Emerging Technologies: AI

We saw in the previous chapter how the rise of AI and its public use marked a real turning point in the world of cybersecurity. AI, despite its advantages, opens the door to a host of abuses in multiple sectors, and digital resilience is one of them. We have rarely seen such a rapid and radical technological revolution, provoking such enthusiasm and, simultaneously, such panic within the public. At all levels, from the individual to the international, discussions surrounding the use of AI are flourishing. The European Parliament states that AI's rapid evolution could have serious consequences as it "could enable malicious actors to produce and spread more disinformation content." It specifies that repercussions could be disastrous, particularly for regions of the world that have limited means to defend themselves. In the United States, the FBI issued an announcement warning the public that "criminals exploit generative artificial intelligence (GenAI) to commit fraud on a larger scale" and with strengthened believability. It brings attention to the fact that these tools make content creation easier and can correct human mistakes that could otherwise have served as warning signs for fraud. This reaction from authorities shows the power that AI can bring to cyberattacks and the danger it represents not only for individuals, but also for the private and public sectors.

How Is AI Used in Cyberattacks?

There is much public debate surrounding this subject, but the fact is that today, a cyberattack cannot be carried out entirely by AI. What AI does is participate in the cyber kill chain to optimize each step individually. The kill chain is the sequence of actions to be performed to deploy a cyberattack from start to finish. Steps may include reconnaissance, code writing, data extraction, and so on. AI is capable of increasing the volume, speed, or precision of each step. However, it is impossible to automate the coordination and sequencing of the different actions using AI without any human intervention. AI is incapable of adapting attacks to the context and the defenses put in place by the victims. Let's examine in detail what AI can be used for.

First, in terms of volume, AI is a real driving force. It allows operations to be deployed at a far larger scale than what could previously be done. Any attack that relies on repetition gains power through the use of AI. Attacks are automated, which means an unprecedented number of devices and individuals are impacted.

Second, AI is an asset in terms of effectiveness and precision. It is capable of bypassing traditional security measures put in place by victims, which are already weak and limited in the case of CSOs. It also launches increasingly sophisticated attacks and, in the case of extortion or manipulation, the personal information that is exploited is becoming more accurate.

AI is also used for content generation: deepfakes (sounds or visuals), fake websites intended to scam users, and increasingly convincing phishing emails. It can also create malware relatively easily. This makes nonprofits even more vulnerable, as their staff is relatively untrained in spotting cyberattacks like phishing or CEO fraud.

When it comes to other types of cyberattacks, AI can simplify tasks such as data collection, reconnaissance, and exploiting system vulnerabilities, for example during the preparation of a ransomware attack. It can also release malware that can then spread within the device and to other devices, without the need for any human intervention.

Societal Consequences and Information Manipulation

In January 2025, the first AI Safety Report was published by 96 AI experts at the request of over 30 countries. The report details the risks that AI represents and the difficulties faced by entities that attempt to counter them.

Among other things, it explores the use of AI for writing news articles, a subject linked to information manipulation. Recent studies have shown an increase in the number of AI-generated articles. They have also shown that its use can reduce content-generation costs by up to 70%. In addition, with this technology becoming more convincing, fewer and fewer individuals are able to spot an article written by AI. The use of AI in information manipulation campaigns is no longer an anomaly; it's now the norm and will continue to develop.

The rise of AI even has effects on content that is not generated by AI, as it creates an atmosphere of widespread skepticism. As AI-generated content becomes more common, researchers also express concern about the erosion of trust in the media by the public. They fear that in this environment, individuals will be more and more suspicious of information in general, whether the messages are correct, involuntarily mistaken, or intentionally false. This leads to new complexity and serious problems for the public debate.

Additional Resources

Builders, `https://protect.ngo/the-builders`, Protect[ngo]

Common Good Cyber Tool Mapping, `https://commongoodcyber.org/cyber-tools`, Common Good Cyber

Common Guidance on Passwords, `https://nonprofitcyber.org/common-guidance-on-passwords`, Nonprofit Cyber

Cyber Resilience Corps, https://www.cybervolunteers.us/en, Protect[ngo] and UC Berkeley Center for Long-Term Cybersecurity

Cyber Solutions Index, https://nonprofitcyber.org/nonprofit-cyber-solutions-index, Nonprofit Cyber

Cybersecurity Toolkits, https://gcatoolkit.org, Global Cyber Alliance

Daily Reports, https://www.shadowserver.org/what-we-do/network-reporting/get-reports, The Shadowserver Foundation

Disinformation Analyst: Hands-on Crash Course, https://www.debunk.org/challenge-page/6a4f0985-cea2-4ba3-8318-deb87fa7d686, Debunk.org

Media Literacy Digest, https://edmo.eu/resources/media-literacy-digest, European Digital Media Observatory

NGO-ISAC, https://ngoisac.org

Project Galileo, https://www.cloudflare.com/galileo, Cloudflare

Ransomware Countermeasures Tracker, https://virtual-routes.org/ransomware-countermeasures-tracker, Virtual Routes

Security Planner, https://securityplanner.consumerreports.org, The Citizen Lab

Spyware Litigation Tracker, https://citizenlab.ca/spyware-litigation-tracker-legal-challenges-and-formal-complaints-related-to-mercenary-spyware, The Citizen Lab

Stop Ransomware, https://www.cisa.gov/stopransomware, U.S. Cybersecurity and Infrastructure Security Agency

Take9, https://pausetake9.org

The Hub for Nonprofit Technology Resources & Insights, https://nethope.org/resources, NetHope

Too much information: A Public Guide, https://firstdraftnews.org/long-form-article/too-much-information, First Draft

Tools to Monitor Disinformation, https://www.disinfo.eu/resources/tools-to-monitor-disinformation, EU DisinfoLab

Refer to Chapter 4 for more detailed information about these tools.

Actions for Resilience: What Can States Do?

Anchor Digital Resilience in Human Rights

States must ensure that all laws, policies, and practices in the digital domain fully comply with international human rights law.

This includes strong and enforceable protections for:

- Privacy and personal data
- Freedom of expression, association, and the press
- Protection from unlawful surveillance

A resilient digital society cannot exist where fundamental rights are weakened in the name of security.

End the Misuse of Surveillance Technologies

The proliferation of spyware and intrusive surveillance tools poses a direct threat to civil society.

States should:

- Prohibit the use of spyware against civil society, journalists, and human rights defenders
- Where exceptional use is claimed, limit it strictly through legality, necessity, proportionality, and independent judicial oversight
- Ensure transparency, accountability, and access to remedy

Security built on fear and opacity ultimately undermines trust and legitimacy.

Ensure Accountability for Cyber Harm

States have a duty not only to protect civil society, but also to respect and enforce international norms in cyberspace.

This requires:

- Upholding norms of responsible state behavior, including the obligation not to conduct or knowingly support cyber operations that harm civilians, civil society, or essential services
- Publicly attributing cyber operations, where credible evidence exists, to their responsible authors, including states, state-controlled entities, or proxies
- Using political attribution, diplomatic measures, and public disclosure as tools to deter further violations and reinforce international norms
- Investigating and prosecuting cybercrime affecting civil society, regardless of borders

Where harmful cyber activity remains unattributed and unpunished, impunity persists—and resilience is weakened.

States should therefore treat responsible, evidence-based political attribution and naming of perpetrators as an essential component of accountability and deterrence, in line with international law and the principles of state responsibility.

Protect Data Without Exclusion

Comprehensive data protection laws must apply to all categories of personal data, including:

(*continued*)

(*continued*)

- Digital identity systems
- Metadata
- Biometric and surveillance data

States should avoid making mandatory digital identification a condition for access to essential public services, as this creates structural risks of exclusion, abuse, and surveillance.

Safeguard Access to Information

States must refrain from practices that restrict access to information, including:

- Internet shutdowns or throttling
- Arbitrary blocking of websites
- Harassment or intimidation of online media and civil society actors

Access to information is indispensable for democratic participation and crisis response.

Engage Civil Society as a Security Partner

Civil society must be recognized as a partner in shaping cybersecurity and digital governance policies.

States should institutionalize inclusive consultation processes, ensuring that those most exposed to digital threats can inform the policies designed to protect them.

Strengthen Institutions Through Training and Ethics

States should invest in training for public officials, law enforcement, and security services on:

- Responsible use of digital tools
- Human-rights-based cybersecurity approaches
- Ethical procurement and deployment of technology

Legitimate security policies require capable and accountable institutions.

Invest in Resilience as a Global Public Good

Digital resilience for civil society is a global public good.

States should:

- Provide sustained financial support to the Common Good Cyber Fund, which strengthens the nonprofit organizations, tools, and infrastructures that underpin global cybersecurity
- Recognize that underfunded civil society creates systemic vulnerabilities with cross-border consequences

Collective investment is essential to closing the global cyber resilience gap and protecting the digital commons.

Commit to International Cooperation

Digital threats do not stop at borders, and international cooperation remains essential. However, cooperation frameworks must not weaken the very actors they aim to protect.

States must:

- Strengthen cooperation by sharing threat intelligence and good practices
- Support confidence-building measures and normative processes at the United Nations

(*continued*)

(continued)

- Approach international cybercrime instruments, including the United Nations Convention Against Cybercrime, with caution and heightened scrutiny

In particular, states should:

- Ensure that cybercrime laws and cooperation mechanisms are narrowly defined, proportionate, and accompanied by strong human-rights safeguards
- Prevent the misuse of cybercrime frameworks to criminalize legitimate civil society activities, including journalism, digital security research, activism, and human rights work
- Recognize that overly broad offenses and procedural powers risk enabling unlawful surveillance, repression, and transnational abuse

International cooperation must strengthen security without legitimizing repression.

No state is resilient alone—but collective security must not come at the expense of fundamental freedoms.

Protecting Civil Society Online Is Not Optional

It is a responsibility—and a test of collective commitment to a secure, open, and rights-respecting digital future.

Actions for Resilience: What Can Philanthropy Do?

Digital Security Is a Prerequisite for Impact

No matter their mission—humanitarian aid, health, climate, education, culture, human rights—foundations rely on CSOs to deliver impact on the ground.

Without Digital Security, No Mission Can Be Delivered Safely or Sustainably

Cyberattacks, data breaches, surveillance, and information manipulation directly disrupt programs, expose beneficiaries, endanger staff and undermine trust. Digital resilience is therefore not an optional add-on, but a core duty of care for every foundation.

Foundations must assume responsibility for the digital protection of the organizations they fund.

Fund Organizational Resilience, Not Only Programs

CSOs require long-term capacity to operate safely and sustainably.

- Fund organizational development and governance, including board oversight, internal controls, and digital risk management.
- Require the implementation of basic cyber hygiene standards and finance their deployment step by step, including essential security tools (secure email, password managers, multi-factor authentication, VPNs, backups).

(*continued*)

(*continued*)

- Provide nonrestricted and flexible funding that allows organizations to allocate resources according to their operational and digital risk exposure.
- Systematically request reporting on cybersecurity improvements and risk reduction enabled by your funding.

Build Digital Skills, Leadership, and Accountability

Cyber resilience must be embedded at the leadership and governance level.

- Finance cybersecurity and digital risk training for staff, senior leadership, and board members.
- Require cybersecurity to be addressed at the governance level and integrated into organizational decision-making.
- Include digital resilience as a formal criterion in grant monitoring, organizational assessments, and renewal decisions.

Enable Civil Society Participation and Collective Leverage

Digital threats are systemic and cross-border; responses must be collective.

- Fund the participation of CSOs in international and multistakeholder forums where cybersecurity, digital governance, and rights are negotiated.
- Support structured exchanges between local and international civil society actors, particularly in global hubs where fragmentation weakens collective resilience.

Strengthen Collective Protection Mechanisms

Individual organizations cannot defend themselves alone.

- Fund specialized CSOs whose mandate is to protect other civil society actors against cyber threats, surveillance, and information manipulation.
- Require and support grantees to use the Cyber Builders program, which delivers free, expert-driven cybersecurity assessments, operational support, and incident response to CSOs at scale.
- Contribute financially to the Common Good Cyber Fund, a pooled, multi-year mechanism that strengthens global public-interest cybersecurity by sustaining nonprofit organizations delivering critical security infrastructure, threat intelligence, incident response, and protection for civil society, journalists, and human rights defenders.
- Fund independent research on cyber threats, digital repression, and information manipulation, and support independent media as pillars of democratic resilience.

Protect People Affected by Cyber Harm

Cyber incidents cause human harm, not only technical disruption.

- Ensure that victims of cyberattacks, surveillance, or prolonged online harassment within CSOs have access to psychological and psychosocial support.
- Treat digital resilience as a duty of care toward people, not merely as a compliance or IT requirement.

(*continued*)

(*continued*)

Shape a Protective Legal and Political Environment

Foundations have influence that extends beyond funding.

- Advocate for laws and public policies addressing digital threats in line with international human rights norms, including protection from cybercrime, unlawful surveillance, and information manipulation.
- Defend freedom of expression, freedom of association, and media freedom as nonnegotiable conditions for a resilient civil society.
- Actively support open, secure, and reliable Internet access for all, recognizing digital connectivity as essential infrastructure for civic action.

Digital resilience is now a prerequisite for civil society to operate, protect beneficiaries, and deliver impact.

By treating cybersecurity as a core funding responsibility—and by investing collectively—foundations directly safeguard their missions, their grantees, and the civic space itself.

Actions for Resilience: What Can CSOs Do?

Making Digital Resilience Mission-Critical—and a Board-Level Responsibility

Cybersecurity is no longer a technical or support function.

It determines whether an organization can operate, protect its people, safeguard beneficiaries, and deliver impact.

Whatever the mandate—humanitarian aid, health, climate, education, culture, or advocacy—without digital security, there is no safe fieldwork, no trusted operations, and no sustainable mission delivery.

Responsibility for digital resilience sits first and foremost with the board of directors.

Boards must ensure that their organizations have the capacity to make sound decisions on data, AI, and cybersecurity. These are not technical matters, but strategic choices that directly affect mission delivery, exposure to risk, legal obligations, reputation, and duty of care.

Boards are accountable for ensuring that:

- Adequate expertise exists—internally or through trusted advisers—to support informed decisions on data, AI, and cyber risk
- Digital risk is treated as an organizational risk, on par with financial, legal, and physical security
- Digital tools, platforms, and data are adopted and governed in line with organizational values, responsibilities, and threat exposure

Digital resilience begins with governance.

(*continued*)

(*continued*)

Establish Leadership Accountability for Cybersecurity

Operational responsibility must be clearly assigned.

- Designate senior leadership responsibility for cybersecurity and digital risk management.
- Integrate cyber risk into organizational strategy, governance discussions, and crisis management planning.
- Ensure alignment between board oversight and executive decision-making on digital and technological issues.

Cyber resilience is a leadership choice before it becomes an operational one.

Build a Security-Aware Organizational Culture

People are the primary targets of cyberattacks—and the primary line of defense.

- Provide regular, mandatory training for leadership and staff on manipulation, fraud, and social engineering, with a focus on decision-making under pressure.
- Institutionalize reflection over urgency: treat unexpected requests and artificial time pressure as warning signals, not calls to act.
- Require systematic verification of identities, instructions, and sources across email, messaging tools, video calls, and social media.
- Ensure that staff who report doubts, mistakes, or incidents are supported, never blamed or stigmatized.

Resilient organizations surface problems early; fragile ones silence them.

Reduce Exposure Through Structural Security Choices

Baseline security is nonnegotiable.

- Enforce multi-factor authentication and strong identity and access management for all users.
- Apply a zero-trust approach: never assume accounts, devices, or networks are safe by default.
- Maintain regular updates, backups, and strict access controls.
- Actively manage what information is shared publicly and operationally.

Treat Domain and Email Impersonation as a Structural Risk

Protecting organizational identity online is essential. Weaknesses in email authentication and domain integrity remain a primary entry point for fraud, targeted compromise, and donor impersonation. These are not edge cases, but systemic risks that directly impact trust and operations.

Assume Accounts Will Be Targeted

Credential theft and account compromise are now among the most common and damaging patterns affecting CSOs.

Leaked credentials, infostealer malware, and account reuse allow attackers to access email, cloud services, and financial tools—often without being detected for long periods. Most organizations become aware of compromises late, if at all, without external monitoring or support.

Digital resilience requires assuming that user accounts will be targeted and designing controls and partnerships accordingly.

(*continued*)

(*continued*)

Prepare for Incidents Before They Happen

Cyber incidents are inevitable. Unprepared organizations pay a higher price.

- Maintain a clear, rehearsed incident response plan that defines roles, escalation paths, and communication responsibilities.
- Isolate incidents quickly, secure compromised accounts, and protect critical services.
- Document incidents systematically.

Build Evidence-Ready Incident Response

For every significant incident, ensure a minimum, structured record: a clear timeline, affected systems, indicators observed, and actions taken. This allows organizations to share usable information with trusted responders, partners, and, where appropriate, authorities, instead of relying on fragmented or ad hoc reporting.

Never pay ransoms or comply with extortion demands.

Prepared organizations recover faster and protect people better.

Engage in Collective Defense and Trusted Networks

No CSO can defend itself alone.

- Use expert-driven collective support programs such as the Cyber Builders, which connect CSOs with vetted cybersecurity professionals to provide free assessments, operational support, and incident response at scale.

- Rely on practical, mission-aware guidance such as the Global Cyber Alliance's NGO Cybersecurity Kit to strengthen baseline protections across teams.
- Actively participate in civil society networks that enable coordination, peer learning, and joint response to digital threats, including:
  - The International Civil Society Centre (ICSC) and its Solidarity Action Network, supporting collective action and mutual assistance when organizations face cyberattacks or civil space restrictions.
  - NetHope, whose Digital Protection programs and information-sharing mechanisms strengthen sector-wide resilience.
- Where available, engage with regional and public initiatives designed to facilitate incident reporting, secure information sharing, and coordination with responders.

Collective defense turns isolated organizations into a resilient ecosystem.

Protect People, Not Only Systems

Cyberattacks are designed to intimidate, exhaust, and isolate.

- Acknowledge the psychological impact of cyber incidents, surveillance, and online harassment on staff and leadership.
- Ensure access to psychosocial support for those affected.
- Treat care for people as a core component of digital resilience.

(*continued*)

(*continued*)

Civil society operates on trust, proximity, and responsibility toward the communities it serves. In an increasingly hostile digital environment, digital resilience is no longer optional.

By placing accountability at the board level, treating cybersecurity as a strategic responsibility, preparing for identity-based threats, and relying on trusted collective mechanisms, CSOs protect their missions, their people—and the civil space itself.

Sources

Amnesty International. "What Is Spyware and What Can You Do to Stay Protected?" December 14, 2023. https://www.amnesty.org/en/latest/campaigns/2023/12/what-is-spyware-and-what-you-can-do-to-stay-protected

The Asia Foundation APAC Cybersecurity Fund. "From Vulnerability to Resilience: Cybersecurity Challenges for MSMEs in the APAC Region." July 2024. https://protect.ngo/resources/cybersecurity-challenges-for-msmes-in-the-apac-region

Baines, Paul. "Ukrainian Propaganda: How Zelensky Is Winning the Information War Against Russia." *The Conversation*, May 11, 2022. https://theconversation.com/ukrainian-propaganda-how-zelensky-is-winning-the-information-war-against-russia-182061

Cervantes, Edgar. "How to Unroot Your Android Phone or Tablet." *Android Authority*, April 10, 2025. https://www.androidauthority.com/how-to-unroot-android-phone-tablet-652905

Cyber Zaintza. "Buenas prácticas frente al ransomware." (n.d.) https://ciberseguridad.euskadi.eus/ciberpedia/

ransomware/buenas-practicas-frente-al-ransomware/webcyb00-contdocu/es

D'Andrea, Ashley. "¿Cómo sé si tengo spyware?" *Keeper*, August 27, 2024. https://www.keepersecurity.com/blog/es/2024/08/27/how-do-i-know-if-i-have-spyware

The DFIR Report. "2021 Year In Review." March 7, 2022. https://thedfirreport.com/2022/03/07/2021-year-in-review

EU DisinfoLab. "We Fight Disinformation Because We Fight for Democracy." April 11, 2025. https://www.disinfo.eu/we-fight-disinformation-because-we-fight-for-democracy

EU DisinfoLab and Logically. *HEAT: Harmful Environment Agendas and Tactics*. June 2025. https://www.disinfo.eu/wp-content/uploads/2025/06/20250623-heat-harmful-environmental-agendas-tactics.pdf

European Commission. "The 2022 Code of Practice on Disinformation."(n.d.)https://digital-strategy.ec.europa.eu/en/policies/code-practice-disinformation

European Parliament. "Disinformation: 10 Steps to Protect Yourself and Others." June 5, 2025. https://www.europarl.europa.eu/topics/en/article/20250603STO28720/disinformation-10-steps-to-protect-yourself-and-others

European Parliament. "Report on Foreign Interference in All Democratic Processes in the European Union, Including Disinformation." May 15, 2023. https://www.europarl.europa.eu/doceo/document/A-9-2023-0187_EN.html

European Union. *Regulation (EU) 2022/2065 of the European Parliament and of the Council of 19 October 2022 on a Single Market for Digital Services and Amending Directive 2000/31/EC (Digital Services Act)*. October 27, 2022. https://eur-lex.europa.eu/legal-content/EN/TXT/?uri=CELEX%3A32022R2065&qid=1763035652397

Europol. "CEO/Business Email Compromise (BEC) Fraud." (n.d.) https://www.europol.europa.eu/cms/sites/default/files/documents/4_ceo-bec_fraud.pdf

Federal Bureau of Investigation. "Public Service Announcement: Criminals Use Generative Artificial Intelligence to Facilitate Financial Fraud." December 3, 2024. https://www.ic3.gov/PSA/2024/PSA241203

García Alarcón, Bárbara. "Fraude del CEO: El engaño que puede vaciar la cuenta de tu pyme." *Instituto Nacional de Ciberseguridad.* July 3, 2025. https://www.incibe.es/empresas/blog/fraude-del-ceo-el-engano-que-puede-vaciar-la-cuenta-de-tu-pyme

Global Interagency Security Forum. "Disinformation and Security Risk Management for NGOs." July 31, 2020. https://gisf.ngo/blogs/disinformation-and-security-risk-management-for-ngos

The Hague Humanity Hub, Stichting the Shadowserver Foundation Europe, Connect2Trust Foundation, and Protect[ngo]. *Cyber Resilience for NGOs: A Collective Intelligence Effort.* November 27, 2024. https://protect.ngo/resources/cyber-resilience-ngos-collective-intelligence-effort

InfoQ Podcast. "GenAI Security: Defending Against Deepfakes and Automated Social Engineering." December 3, 2025. https://www.infoq.com/podcasts/defending-against-deepfakes-automated-engineering/?utm_medium=email&_hsenc=p2ANqtz-8Ukebh8ED1pk0W7nMsoUt1hbKoKD1eRVIlXmeHv4lJ2w4T2zJ7rmP3qJYQVYCV9poJkvCP4qBHAFnOwhBzYSM3EAmm8t2aRxqil3IHaPIg4s2j03w&_hsmi=395068634&utm_content=395068634&utm

Instituto Nacional de Ciberseguridad. "¿Conocías el término 'jailbreaking' o 'rooting'?" (n.d.) https://www.incibe.es/ciudadania/blog/conocias-el-termino-jailbreaking-o-rooting

Instituto Nacional de Ciberseguridad. "Privacidad, identidad digital y reputación online." (n.d.) https://www.incibe.es/index.php/ciudadania/tematicas/privacidad

Lemos, Robert. "Pegasus Spyware Targets Jordanian Civil Society in Wide-Ranging Attacks." *Dark Reading*, February 5, 2024. https://www.darkreading.com/vulnerabilities-threats/pegasus-spyware-targets-jordanian-civil-society

LISA Institute. "Fraude del CEO: qué es, modus operandi y consejos preventivos." (n.d.) https://www.lisainstitute.com/blogs/blog/fraude-del-ceo-que-es-modus-operandi-consejos?srsltid=AfmBOoqC4gksGSJ3mImchkr3Dto3TDs3WvLBoN1pfSRVOLiR1FxZJUzZ

Mapping Media Freedom. "Press Freedom Fact Sheet: Spyware and Surveillance." (n.d.) https://www.mfrr.eu/wp-content/uploads/2025/11/Soopyware-Fact-Sheet-October-2025-Upd.pdf

McMurdo, Torey. "Ukraine Has Been Winning the Messaging Wars. It's Been Preparing for Years." *The Washington Post*, March 28, 2022. https://www.washingtonpost.com/politics/2022/03/28/russia-ukraine-propaganda-misinformation-media-zelensky

Pascual, Manuel G. "Why Russia Has Failed to Win the Cyberwar in Ukraine." *El País*, February 14, 2023. https://english.elpais.com/international/2023-02-14/why-russia-has-failed-to-win-the-cyberwar-in-ukraine.html

Pichurov, Todor. "7 señales tempranas clave de ataques de ransomware." *SpyHunter*, February 10, 2025. https://www.spyhunter.com/shm/es/senales-tempranas-de-ataques-de-ransomware

Protect[ngo]. "NGOs Serving Humanity at Risk: Cyber Threats Affecting International Geneva." December 7, 2023. https://protect.ngo/resources/cyberpeace-analytical-reportngos-serving-humanity-at-risk-cyber-threats-affecting-international-geneva

Protect[ngo]. "Platform #Ukraine, Attack Details." (n.d.) https://cyberconflicts.protect.ngo/threats/attack-details

Protect[ngo]. "Ransomware: Follow the Threat Actor." October 2025. https://protect.ngo/resources/ransomware-follow-the-threat-actor

Protect[ngo]. "Understanding Nexus Operations: Where Cyberattacks and Disinformation Converge." September 1, 2025. https://protect.ngo/news/understanding-nexus-operations-where-cyberattacks-and-disinformation-converge

Pulido, Laetitia. "Menaces de désinformation contre les organisations de la société civile." *University of Lausanne*, June 2025

Segura, Christian. "Ukraine Claims Russia Uses Its Cooperation with China to Carry Out Cyberattacks." *El País*, February 12, 2024. https://english.elpais.com/international/2024-02-12/ukraine-claims-russia-uses-its-cooperation-with-china-to-carry-out-cyberattacks.html

Smalley, Suzanne. "Spyware Maker Is Hijacking Diplomatic Efforts to Limit Commercial Hacking, Civil Society Warns." *The Record*, February 2, 2026. https://therecord.media/spyware-maker-pall-mall-process-reputation

Tarun, Renee. "When It Comes to Ransomware, Don't Forget the Basics." *Fortinet*, March 10, 2022. https://www.fortinet.com/blog/ciso-collective/when-it-comes-to-ransomware-dont-forget-the-basics

TechSoup Talks. "Digital Security: Safety Is Not Optional, with Stéphane Duguin." YouTube Video, July 14, 2025. https://www.youtube.com/watch?v=bRtK7amRwzg

Temin, Davia. "8 Ways to Protect Your Reputation When Targeted by Disinformation." *Forbes*, July 6, 2025. https://www.forbes.com/sites/daviatemin/2025/07/06/8-ways-to-protect-your-reputation-when-targeted-by-disinformation

UK National Cyber Security Centre. "Phishing Attacks: Defending Your Organisation." (n.d.) https://www.ncsc.gov.uk/guidance/phishing

UK National Cyber Security Centre. "Ransomware: Threat Methodology." (n.d.) https://www.ncsc.gov.uk/collection/ncsc-annual-review-2021/the-threat/ransomware-threat-methodology

Union of Concerned Scientists. "How to Stop Disinformation." April 1, 2022. https://www.ucs.org/resources/how-stop-disinformation

Unwanted Witness Uganda. *Surveillance/Spyware: An Impediment to Civil Society, HRDs and Journalists in East & Southern Africa.* June 6, 2025. https://www.unwantedwitness.org/wp-content/uploads/2025/06/Report-06.06.2025-FINAL.pdf

US Cybersecurity and Infrastructure Security Agency. "Protecting Against Malicious Code." November 19, 2019. https://www.cisa.gov/news-events/news/protecting-against-malicious-code

US Cybersecurity and Infrastructure Security Agency. "Recognizing and Avoiding Spyware." September 27, 2019. https://www.cisa.gov/news-events/news/recognizing-and-avoiding-spyware

US Cybersecurity and Infrastructure Security Agency. "Understanding Anti-Virus Software." September 27, 2019. https://www.cisa.gov/news-events/news/understanding-anti-virus-software

World Health Organization. "How to Report Misinformation Online." (n.d.) https://www.who.int/campaigns/connecting-the-world-to-combat-coronavirus/how-to-report-misinformation-online

CHAPTER

3

Accountability: State Responsibility and the Actors Behind the Attacks

June 2024. My first instinct upon entering the main chamber of the United Nations Security Council in New York was nothing out of the ordinary. Caught in a perfect mix of excitement and intense stress, I had a very human reaction: I called my mother. I had the phone in my hand when the Master of Ceremonies interrupted me. He spoke very quickly, explained the protocol, told me where I should sit, now, later, when to move, and in which direction. He handed me a wooden plaque engraved with my name, and five minutes later, following the South Korean presiding officer, Cho Tae-yul, and the UN Secretary-General,

António Guterres, I addressed the nation-states. My speech that day was simple—if you are reading these lines, you will soon be capable of delivering a similar one. I made sure to emphasize the convergence of cyberattacks and information manipulation. This is a systemic threat to any ideal of international peace and security.

In this raging conflict, I talked about the frontlines, those held by civil society. I talked about the organizations that provide for our basic needs in geographies and sectors where neither public authorities nor private companies dare to intervene.

Others spoke up, one after another, and I was still gathering my thoughts, wondering if I'd said everything I needed to, when I heard the representative from the Russian Federation. He denied any information manipulation activity and maintained that his country was at the forefront of the fight against cybercrime. This made me think of my mother again. I made a mental note to thank her for steering me toward a career where I didn't have to listen to this kind of thing all day long.

The denial itself was predictable. What struck me was how easily reality could be rewritten from behind a nameplate and a microphone. In diplomatic spaces, attribution is negotiable, responsibility elastic, and harm a matter of interpretation. States formally recognize their responsibility to ensure stability in cyberspace, yet too often fail to uphold it—either by action, omission, or convenient ambiguity.

For CSOs, none of this is abstract. Attacks have timelines, perpetrators, costs, and aftermaths. The gap between the role states claim to play and the stability they actually provide directly shapes who absorbs the risk. Civil society is not collateral damage in this landscape. It is the frontline—and too often the buffer zone. In practice, when states fail to enforce, fail to cooperate, or choose ambiguity, they externalize cyber risk onto organizations that were never designed to carry it: NGOs, journalists, human rights defenders, community networks, and the people who depend on them. That transfer of risk is not an accident. It is the predictable outcome of inaction.

Keeping the peace in cyberspace is therefore not a single problem with a single fix. It is a multidimensional challenge—technical, legal, and political—made worse by fragmented standards and inconsistent incentives.

The Premise: States Have a Double Duty

This chapter is normative. It does not ask whether states "care." It states what they owe, and it judges them by whether they deliver it.

In cyberspace, states have a double responsibility. First, a responsibility to protect—through operational capacity, trained investigators and prosecutors, credible reporting routes, and international cooperation that works at the pace of modern attacks. Second, a responsibility to do no harm—not to hide behind "national security" to justify the use of cyberspace as an unaccountable space for repression, excessive surveillance, intimidation, or manipulation. These duties are inseparable. A state that claims to protect while quietly undermining rights is not protecting; it is redistributing harm.

This reflects the baseline that states themselves have repeatedly affirmed in multilateral discussions on responsible behavior in cyberspace: international law applies, voluntary norms exist, and implementation and capacity building are essential. The challenge has never been the absence of principles. It has been their translation into practice.

The uncomfortable reality is that states often seek the language of protection without the discipline of restraint. They favor cooperation when it serves enforcement, and opacity when it serves control. Cybersecurity becomes a governance tool rather than a protection framework. The question, therefore, is not whether norms exist, but whether they are operationalized in ways that reduce harm for those most exposed—or merely manage them.

The Temptation: Law as Theater

There is a reflex that states share across ideologies: when faced with an inconvenient reality, they legislate. Not always to solve the problem—often to demonstrate that they have responded. The performance is familiar: a new strategy, a new coordination mechanism, a new convention, a "historic step." But cybercrime and cyber aggression do not respond to ceremonies. They respond to friction.

The test is therefore operational and pragmatic. When states point to frameworks—regional, international, or national—four questions matter. Does the framework protect victims without increasing the cost of reporting? Does it raise the probability of investigators identifying and constraining perpetrators? Does it constrain abuse by the state itself when security arguments are invoked? And does it reduce impunity, rather than repackage it? A framework that increases power without accountability is not protection; it is risk transfer.

In the cyber domain, "risk transfer" is not theoretical. It happens when reporting becomes legally risky for victims, when cooperation mechanisms can be turned into surveillance pipelines, or when broad offences allow states to criminalize the very actors who help keep the ecosystem safe—journalists, researchers, and CSOs. Laws that are designed to fight cybercrime can, without safeguards, become tools of repression, and that is precisely how legitimacy erodes.

The Duty to Protect: What It Actually Means

A duty to protect is not a moral aspiration. It is a set of operational consequences.

It begins with reporting mechanisms that do not punish disclosure. Many CSOs remain silent for rational reasons: fear of reputational damage, donor uncertainty, legal exposure, or simply the risk of becoming a repeat target. Protection means making reporting safe, meaningful, and useful.

It extends to evidence. Digital traces decay quickly. Infrastructure shifts. Cooperation slows. "We will investigate" is meaningless if investigative capacity cannot move at the speed of the threat. And even when evidence exists, a second clock matters: the time of justice is not the time of response. Legal certainty can take months or years; victims need containment, continuity, and remedy now. The gap between those clocks is one of the quiet engines of impunity.

These dynamics become concrete during incidents. In recent years, a major humanitarian organization operating across multiple countries was hit by a ransomware attack while field operations were ongoing. The incident became public through an extortion leak, not through any state warning or support mechanism. Systems were partially encrypted, sensitive data exfiltrated, crisis management activated overnight. Leadership was diverted from program delivery, partners demanded assurances, and staff continued operating amid uncertainty about exposure. The burden of response rested almost entirely on the organization itself.

Over time, investigations into ransomware campaigns targeting public-interest sectors reveal a consistent pattern: success depends less on technical sophistication than on jurisdictional fragmentation and state inaction. Known infrastructures remain untouched. Dependencies are tolerated. Disruption is episodic. Protection, in other words, remains systemic in name only.

The harm does not stop with recovery. CSOs are forced into prolonged evidence production—reconstructing timelines, preserving artifacts, navigating providers, lawyers, donors, and staff trauma—often exhausting their technical, legal, and emotional capacity long before justice becomes realistic. In most cases, even when a culprit is suspected, the question that matters to victims remains unanswered: what consequence follows, and who will carry the cost until it does?

The Duty to Do No Harm: The Part States Avoid

The second duty—do no harm—is the one states address most cautiously, precisely because it constrains them.

Promising to fight cybercrime is politically easy. Credibly constraining surveillance, spyware, and coercive cyber capabilities is not. Yet a state cannot claim legitimacy in protecting civil society while simultaneously expanding the spaces in which harm is enabled through ambiguous laws and weak oversight.

Repeated investigations have shown how intrusive surveillance tools have been used against activists, journalists, and CSO staff, often without interaction or warning. The damage is not merely digital. Networks collapse. Sources are exposed. Activities cease. Trust evaporates.

When responses are limited to denial, legality claims, or procedural reviews, the message to civil society is clear: protection is conditional, restraint optional. And accountability often fails at step zero: institutions—public and private—can be hesitant to acknowledge incidents at all, fearing reputational loss, political backlash, or legal exposure. Silence becomes an operating practice. That silence does not reduce harm; it simply shifts it.

The UN Cybercrime Convention: A Perfect Example of "Framework vs. Operationalization"

If you want a case study of how the existence of a framework does not guarantee protection, the UN Cybercrime Convention offers a clear example.

On paper, the Convention promises stronger cooperation, harmonization, and faster access to evidence. In practice, its breadth and weak safeguards risk expanding state powers without measurably improving outcomes for victims. This concern is shared across civil society, parts of the cybersecurity industry, and human rights experts.

The issue is straightforward. A framework that broadens authority without ensuring accountability and remedy does not close protection gaps—it reshapes them. For CSOs, such instruments risk increasing exposure while leaving the likelihood of justice largely unchanged.

This is not opposition to international cooperation. It is a reminder that cooperation that prioritizes capability over accountability does not equal protection. The real test remains operational: does it change what happens when an incident occurs?

The warning signs are familiar: vague offences, expansive procedural powers, and weak safeguards can be repurposed against legitimate civil society activity—including journalism, digital security research, activism, and human rights work. In our own institutional practice, we have warned that overly broad scope and vague provisions risk enabling surveillance abuses, threatening civil liberties, and jeopardizing cybersecurity research.

International cooperation must strengthen security without legitimizing repression. Otherwise, the framework itself becomes a risk multiplier.

Responsibility Without Attribution: The Trick States Rely On

In cyberspace, attribution is not a single act, but a layered process. Technical attribution focuses on indicators, infrastructure, tools, and patterns associated with an incident. Political attribution reflects a state's decision to assign responsibility—publicly or privately—often based on intelligence and strategic calculation. Legal attribution is narrower and more demanding: it requires that specific legal criteria be met before state responsibility can be engaged under international law.

These layers rarely align. Technical findings may be strong, and political signals explicit, while legal responsibility remains formally uninvoked. The result is a persistent responsibility gap: attacks are widely understood, sometimes even acknowledged, yet rarely translated into enforceable legal consequences. This gap is not incidental. It shapes attacker behavior.

History also shows a harder truth: attribution is not always in the victim's interest. Even when a state is "pointed to" quickly, what follows can be damaging rather than helpful—especially when claims are premature, politically convenient, or based on weak evidence.

In June 2017, malware infected the systems of many Ukrainian companies and infrastructures, spreading through widely used accounting software. The malware impacted companies, but also banks, government websites, and the Kharkiv airport in Ukraine, and then spread worldwide. Global losses were estimated at USD 10 billion. The attack interrupted essential functions such as transportation and pharmaceutical production. Many affected entities turned to insurers to contain damage and rebuild. Insurers, taking advantage of the rapid narrative that this was an act of war, invoked war exclusions and refused to pay. Years of litigation followed. An American pharmaceutical company eventually succeeded against multiple insurers in 2024—almost seven years after the incident. That path is expensive in money, time, and institutional energy. Large corporations may sustain it. CSOs rarely can. And the attribution narrative itself remained contested over time. In cases like this, attribution does not serve victims; it can deepen their disadvantage.

This is why "naming" cannot be treated as the endpoint of accountability. It is not only about having a name. It is about knowing what to do with it so that it leads to actual outcomes: justice, reparations, remedy, or meaningful deterrence. The difference matters.

The Standards Problem: Why Accountability Collapses Before It Starts

Another sizeable challenge is more basic: the absence of coherent and unified standards. There are no consistent international standards for evidence, no agreed approach to handling faulty attribution, and no coherent, shared terminology. Multiple models coexist, producing diffuse, discordant, and hard-to-compare conclusions. This fragmentation is not merely confusing; it is strategically exploitable. Results that cannot be compared can be dismissed, and conclusions produced by non-state actors can be invalidated by states on procedural grounds rather than substantive ones.

If accountability depends on evidence, then evidence must be legible. If accountability depends on harm, then harm must be measurable. This is where the accountability debate has historically failed: the ecosystem has produced abundant technical detail, but struggled to produce consistent, scalable ways to measure harm beyond downtime and financial loss. Our own work has repeatedly confronted this gap: cyber impacts are often measured only in technical terms—downtime, financial loss, breached data—missing the wider harm to people and societies.

Harm Methodology: Measuring What Matters to Make Accountability Possible

To bridge this gap, Protect·ngo developed the Harm Methodology: a framework focusing on the human impact of cyberattacks. It was designed to make harm measurable, comparable, and usable across cases—so that accountability can be pursued on an evidence-led basis rather than on scattered signals.

The core premise is simple: if we cannot measure harm, we cannot manage threats, compare cases, or credibly argue for responsibility and remedy. Technical metrics alone—files exfiltrated, systems encrypted, financial losses—do not capture the harm caused to individuals, communities, civil society, or international stability.

The Harm Methodology distinguishes between four levels of harm:

- Individual harm, affecting personal safety, privacy, dignity, physical or psychological well-being
- Organizational harm, affecting an organization's operations, confidentiality, governance, and duty of care

- Societal harm, affecting trust, essential services, civic space, and community resilience
- International harm, affecting cross-border stability, escalation dynamics, and international peace and security

Its strategic objective is to identify how to measure and assess harm starting from a single incident across multiple indicators and categories, in order to increase knowledge of human costs and influence policy, accountability, and resilience efforts. This includes indicators related to physical and psychological harms, and it leverages Protect^{ngo}'s long-term analysis of cyberattacks against healthcare since June 2020 and monitoring of cyberattacks linked to armed conflict.

The framework relies on principles such as adaptability and transparency: it is designed to be usable even when data is incomplete, and to evolve as new threat patterns and new forms of harm emerge.

Why does this matter for accountability? Because it changes what can be argued, and what can be enforced. When harm is described only as "technical impact," accountability discussions default to technical debates about sophistication, tradecraft, and attribution uncertainty—domains where victims are structurally disadvantaged and where states can stall. When harm is measured in human terms—across individual, organizational, societal, and international layers—accountability can be grounded in outcomes that matter to law, policy, and governance. It also becomes possible to compare incidents, identify patterns, and demonstrate that certain behaviors produce predictable human consequences, making denial, minimization, and selective enforcement harder to sustain.

This is not a substitute for legal attribution. It is an enabling layer. It turns fragmented incident narratives into coherent, reusable, legally meaningful information, so that when responsibility is debated, it is debated on foundations that are consistent, comparable, and oriented toward remedy.

The Role of Civil Society: Contributing to Accountability Ecosystems

There is, however, a role that civil society can play collectively, not as an enforcement authority, but as a contributor to accountability ecosystems. When organizations affected by cyber incidents align their practices around data preservation, incident documentation, and basic forensic hygiene, they increase the likelihood that attacks can be analyzed, correlated, and understood beyond isolated cases.

This does not mean every organization becomes an investigator, nor does it shift responsibility away from states. Rather, it points to the value of networked approaches: shared standards for incident data, secure mechanisms for pooling indicators, and cooperation with trusted technical and legal intermediaries. Within such networks, individual organizations contribute fragments; together, they help form patterns.

Over time, this collective discipline can lower the evidentiary barrier that too often blocks accountability. It strengthens the technical and methodological foundation on which political and legal processes may eventually rely. The objective is not to prove responsibility alone, but to ensure that when responsibility is debated, it is debated on the basis of coherent, reusable, legally meaningful information rather than scattered signals and exhausted victims.

When States Fail: How Impunity Becomes a Policy Choice

States fail civil society through direct harm, selective enforcement, and performative regulation.

Ransomware persistence illustrates this vividly. Criminal ecosystems regenerate not because they are invisible, but because disruption is inconsistent and often politically inconvenient. Over time, tolerance becomes equilibrium.

Cybercrime thrives not only because of technical opportunity, but because of structural constraints on enforcement. Traditional models of law enforcement rely on a stable relationship between offender, victim, and territory. In cyberspace, that triangle is broken. Attacks are conducted remotely, across multiple jurisdictions, through infrastructure that shifts faster than legal cooperation mechanisms can respond.

Where states lack the operational capacity to investigate, preserve evidence, and cooperate across borders at scale, criminal ecosystems adapt. They do not merely exploit loopholes; they reorganize around them. Over time, inconsistency in enforcement signals becomes a form of tolerance, and tolerance becomes predictability. It is this predictability—not anonymity alone—that sustains large-scale cyber extortion and criminal services.

Political calculation deepens this pattern. When an attack is deployed by a state, governments can be hesitant to publicly assign responsibility out of fear of destabilizing relations, triggering escalation, or inviting retaliation. And even when the actor is non-state, linking it to a host jurisdiction can increase tensions between governments. Attribution, even when backed by proof, becomes a political decision, not simply an evidentiary one.

The cost is borne by civil society—and beyond it, by beneficiaries. When CSOs are disrupted, it is vulnerable communities who lose services, confidentiality, and continuity.

What "Responsibility" Should Look Like When Operationalized

For more than two decades, states have invested diplomatic energy in defining norms of responsible behavior in cyberspace. International law was affirmed as applicable. Voluntary norms were adopted. Capacity building was emphasized. On paper, an architecture of responsibility exists.

The failure lies in translation.

Norms without resources, institutions, and accountability mechanisms do not alter outcomes. For CSOs, the distance between what states endorse internationally and what they implement domestically is precisely where exposure accumulates.

That gap has also revealed another dynamic: when states stall at the operational level, others sometimes move.

CSOs, philanthropic actors, and parts of the cybersecurity community have increasingly recognized that fragmentation and underfunding are structural failures. Through the CEO-level call launched under the Beyond125 initiative, they reframed cybersecurity for CSOs as a matter of public interest—a common good—rather than a charitable concern.

That mobilization produced the Common Good Cyber Fund, a mechanism designed to finance cybersecurity capacity at scale. Importantly, it created an entry point for states. Today, a group of governments—including the United Kingdom, Australia, Canada, and the Netherlands—support the Fund as part of a pooled donor model.

This matters because it demonstrates that responsibility does not move only top-down. When civil society organizes, aligns its narrative, and articulates needs in systemic terms, it can trigger solutions of scale.

But accountability cannot be outsourced to philanthropy, international organizations, or the private sector. These actors can help operationalize standards, fund public-interest infrastructure, and constrain abusive markets. They can help counter the imbalance between states, multinationals, and civil society. Yet their role must complement—never replace—the core duty of states: to protect, to restrain, and to ensure consequence.

So what does this mean for CSOs? Do not underestimate the power of numbers. Fragmented appeals are easy to ignore; coordinated demands are not. When civil society shifts from isolated vulnerability to collective pressure, it gains the capacity to catalyze systemic change, including sustained funding. Responsibility must be demanded from states, but it must also be organized.

Opening the Door: The Attacker Ecosystem and Why Accountability Fails

If responsibility is the terrain, attackers are the actors who exploit it. Too often, the public story collapses into a single word—"hackers." That word is convenient, but it is wrong. It hides incentives, masks structure, and makes the threat feel random when it is anything but.

What targets civil society today is not a collection of isolated individuals. It is an ecosystem: adaptive, networked, and shaped by what law enforcement and diplomacy can or cannot do at scale. Under pressure, parts of this ecosystem fragment, multiply, and reconstitute themselves; the underlying economy persists.

Beyond Caricature: Who Sits in the Ecosystem

From the perspective of a CSO, the most useful starting point is not labels, but logics of action. The ecosystem includes:

- Profit-driven criminal actors, who treat access and data as commodities and build "crime-as-a-service" supply chains
- Access and data brokers, who specialize in acquiring and selling entry points and datasets to other criminals
- Influence-oriented operators, whose objective is intimidation, disruption, or narrative control rather than direct financial return (often overlapping with criminal tactics when it works)
- Hybrid and state-linked actors, who can leverage criminal markets, stolen data, and access services for espionage, coercion, or broader strategic agendas
- Opportunists, who exploit moments of crisis, visibility, or reduced defensive capacity

The key point is that these categories are porous. A dataset stolen for profit can become leverage for coercion. Access sold by a broker can enable ransomware, fraud, or intelligence collection. Europol's Internet Organised Crime Threat Assessment (IOCTA) frames data not only as a target but as a means and a commodity—fuel that powers multiple crime types and enables further exploitation.

This porosity becomes even harder to manage in armed conflict. The Russian invasion of Ukraine has shown that cyberattacks can be integral to warfare, and that the boundary between state and non-state actors is increasingly porous. Hacktivists and volunteer collectives play active roles; "cyber forces" can form rapidly out of necessity; and their legal status can remain ambiguous. The IT Army of Ukraine is a useful illustration of this ambiguity: neither civilian nor military; neither public nor private; neither local nor international; neither clearly legal nor illegal. Such actors make accountability harder, and they give states room to deny implication.

Predictability over Invisibility: How Attackers Actually Decide

Many defenders assume attackers win by being invisible. Increasingly, attackers win by being predictably unconstrained.

The cybercriminal economy is built around repeated acquisition and exploitation of data and access, where offenders diversify platforms, use end-to-end encrypted channels for transactions, and adapt quickly under pressure. This is not the behavior of actors who fear being noticed. It is the behavior of actors who have learned that being noticed rarely translates into meaningful consequence.

In that environment, civil society becomes structurally attractive. CSOs often hold high-leverage data (beneficiaries, partners, testimony, locations), depend on trust and continuity, and operate across borders while protection remains uneven. When state cooperation is slow, when enforcement is fragmented, and when legal responsibility is rarely operationalized, the ecosystem reads the signal and prices it in.

The Supply Chain Model: Attacks as a Division of Labor

The most important shift for CSOs to grasp is that many attacks now follow a division of labor. A thriving part of the ecosystem revolves around selling access to compromised systems and accounts, and initial access brokers increasingly advertise these services as an entry point into victim systems. Social engineering is prevalent and increasingly amplified by generative AI and large language models, which can tailor communications and automate criminal processes.

You do not need to know the names of tools to understand what this means: the attacker ecosystem is increasingly modular. One actor specializes in getting in. Another in extracting value. Another in laundering or monetizing. This modularity makes the ecosystem resilient: it can replace components faster than institutions can dismantle them.

AI sharpens this resilience in a specific way: it often optimizes speed, scale, and plausibility without changing the underlying nature of an operation. Except in some edge cases (such as deepfakes), it is almost impossible to detect AI use with complete certainty. That makes malicious use harder to prove, and accountability harder to assign, particularly when responsibility already depends on standards and intent thresholds that lag behind operational reality.

Why Attribution Alone Does Not Change the Game

Attribution matters—but only if it changes incentives.

The IOCTA's framing helps clarify the problem: when the underground economy is built on the trade of access and data, and when actors can rebrand and resurface as marketplaces shift, naming alone rarely disrupts the underlying business model. The gap between technical understanding and legal consequence becomes, for attackers, a stable feature of the operating environment.

This is also where contemporary scholarship is useful without being legalistic. Work on cyber conflict and cybercrime as national security problems emphasizes that attackers thrive not simply on anonymity, but on institutional and political constraints that prevent consistent disruption.

The Game CSOs Are Forced to Play—and How to Stop Playing It Alone

Within this ecosystem, CSOs are inserted into a game whose rules they did not set:

- Pressure is applied faster than cooperation moves.
- Evidence exists before consequence does.
- The burden of continuity falls on victims, not on the system.

The implication is not that CSOs should become investigators or replace states. It is that accountability is increasingly an ecosystem problem, and ecosystem problems require ecosystem responses. The more civil society is isolated, the more attackers can treat each incident as a one-off. The more civil society can connect incidents—through trusted intermediaries, shared standards for incident data, and pooled indicators—the harder it becomes for the ecosystem to hide behind fragmentation.

This is why initiatives that combine research, convening, and practical support, such as those developed within networks like Protect·ngo or Virtual Routes, matter: they help translate an abstract understanding of attacker ecosystems into collective defensive capacity without requiring every organization to become a technical specialist.

The next step is to turn this diagnosis into leverage—practical measures that help CSOs reduce exposure, recover faster, and raise the cost of attacks through collective resilience and targeted accountability.

Actions for Accountability: What Can States Do?

Accountability is not a declaration. It is an operational responsibility.

States play a decisive role in shaping whether accountability in cyberspace remains aspirational or becomes enforceable. Protecting civil society requires more than norms and statements: it requires consistent action, restraint, and consequences.

Translate Cyber Norms into Operational Obligations

States have repeatedly affirmed that international law applies in cyberspace and that norms of responsible behavior exist.

Accountability begins when these commitments are translated into domestic law, institutional mandates, and operational practice.

States should:

- Integrate international cyber norms into national legal frameworks, doctrines, and mandates
- Assign clear institutional responsibility for implementation across law enforcement, prosecution, intelligence, and diplomatic services
- Measure success not by compliance on paper, but by reductions in harm, impunity, and exposure for civil society

Norms that do not change outcomes do not deter abuse.

Enforce the Duty to Protect Across Borders

CSOs are transnational; accountability must be as well.

States must:

- Investigate cybercrime affecting civil society regardless of where perpetrators, infrastructure, or victims are located
- Treat jurisdictional fragmentation as a governance failure, not an excuse for inaction
- Prioritize cross-border cooperation in cases affecting public-interest organizations, journalists, and humanitarian actors

Failure to investigate and prosecute cyber harm is itself a form of tolerance.

Treat Omission and Tolerance as Accountability Failures

Accountability cannot depend solely on proving intent or attribution at the highest political threshold.

States should:

- Recognize omission, inaction, and tolerated activity as relevant elements of responsibility
- Act when malicious cyber ecosystems operate openly and repeatedly within known jurisdictions
- Use disruption, sanctions, legal action, and diplomatic pressure against infrastructures and services that enable repeated harm

Predictable inaction creates predictable abuse.

(*continued*)

(*continued*)

Use Attribution Responsibly and Consistently

Attribution is not symbolic. It is a deterrence tool.

States should:

- Conduct responsible, evidence-based technical and political attribution where credible evidence exists
- Coordinate attribution with legal, diplomatic, and economic measures that raise costs for perpetrators
- Avoid selective or instrumental attribution driven by geopolitical convenience

Constrain State Cyber Power Through Law and Oversight

A state cannot claim to protect civil society while expanding unaccountable cyber capabilities.

States must:

- Ensure that surveillance, intrusion, and data-access powers are grounded in clear law, strict necessity, and proportionality
- Establish independent oversight and effective remedies for abuse
- Prohibit the use of cyber tools against civil society actors, journalists, and human rights defenders

Prevent Frameworks from Becoming Vehicles for Abuse

International cooperation instruments must strengthen protection—not expand repression.

States should:

- Apply heightened scrutiny to cybercrime laws and cooperation mechanisms
- Prevent vague offences and excessive procedural powers from being used against legitimate civil society activity
- Ensure strong safeguards for freedom of expression, research, journalism, and digital security work

Support Accountability Ecosystem

Accountability in cyberspace is an ecosystem challenge.

States should:

- Support mechanisms that enable civil society to document incidents, preserve evidence, and share information securely
- Fund independent technical and legal intermediaries that contribute to attribution and accountability processes
- Recognize that collective, networked approaches lower evidentiary barriers and strengthen enforcement

Invest in Accountability as a Public Good

Accountability does not emerge spontaneously; it must be financed.

(*continued*)

(*continued*)

States should:

- Provide sustained support to the Common Good Cyber Fund and similar pooled mechanisms
- Finance public-interest cybersecurity, data preservation, and accountability infrastructure
- Recognize that underfunded accountability creates systemic risk far beyond national borders

Impunity is cheaper—until its costs are externalized onto society.

Actions for Accountability: What Can Philanthropy Do?

Accountability requires infrastructure—and infrastructure requires funding. For civil society, accountability does not fail because principles are unclear, but because the conditions to operationalize them rarely exist. Philanthropy is therefore not a peripheral actor: it is often the difference between accountability remaining theoretical or becoming possible.

Fund Accountability as Shared Capacity, Not as Emergency Response

Accountability cannot be improvised after harm occurs—especially by organizations with no internal cyber or legal expertise.

Donors should:

- Fund standing, shared capacities for incident documentation, evidence preservation, legal triage, and coordination, rather than one-off crisis grants
- Support collective mechanisms that operate across organizations and sectors, such as Common Good Cyber and the joint action launched under the Beyond125 initiative
- Recognize accountability infrastructure as public-interest digital infrastructure, not administrative overhead

(*continued*)

(*continued*)

What individual CSOs cannot sustain alone must exist somewhere, collectively.

Invest in Organizational Maturity

Most CSOs will never build internal cyber teams—and they should not be expected to.

What philanthropy can realistically enable is baseline technical and organizational maturity, so that organizations are not structurally excluded from accountability processes.

Donors should:

- Fund long-term organizational development that improves basic cyber hygiene, decision-making under incident pressure, and institutional memory
- Support the integration of accountability-relevant practices (documentation, escalation pathways, harm awareness) into governance and management, not only IT
- Understand maturity as the ability to engage safely with external support—not as technical self-sufficiency

Protect Grantees Who Engage in Accountability Processes

Seeking accountability is not neutral. It can trigger legal, political, financial, and security retaliation.

Donors should:

- Provide flexible, rapid funding to cover legal, technical, and security costs linked to incidents or follow-on consequences

- Stand behind grantees facing pressure, harassment, loss of funding, or litigation linked to cyber incidents
- Avoid donor-imposed disclosure or reporting requirements that increase exposure without increasing protection

Strengthen Independent Accountability Intermediaries

CSOs cannot confront states, criminal ecosystems, or surveillance markets alone—and should not be forced to choose between silence and self-exposure.

Donors should:

- Fund specialized, independent intermediaries that provide forensic, legal, and strategic accountability support across cases and sectors
- Sustain research and analysis that connects incidents into patterns of responsibility, tolerance, and omission
- Support secure platforms and trusted networks that enable correlation, not publication

Align Philanthropy with Enforcement Pathways, Not Only Awareness

Awareness without consequence changes little.

Donors should:

- Prioritize initiatives that plausibly contribute to attribution, disruption, remedy, or constraint—even indirectly

(*continued*)

(*continued*)

- Move beyond "capacity building" framed exclusively as training or tooling, when it is disconnected from accountability outcomes
- Require that protection efforts articulate how risk reduction connects to responsibility

Use Philanthropic Leverage to Defend the Accountability Space

Philanthropy is not neutral capital. It has institutional, political, and narrative power.

Donors should:

- Publicly defend independent investigation, journalism, and research when they face legal or political attacks
- Speak out against the misuse of cybercrime, counter-terrorism, or national security frameworks that suppress accountability
- Support norms, institutions, and practices that **constrain power**, rather than expand it without oversight

Civil society does not need philanthropy to "save" it. It needs philanthropy to stop reproducing fragility. Funding isolated tools, short-term fixes, or individual excellence does not produce accountability. Funding shared infrastructure, organizational maturity, and joint action does.

Accountability emerges when civil society is no longer forced to choose between silence and self-destruction—and when those who benefit from its work accept responsibility for the conditions under which that work can be defended.

Actions for Accountability: What Can CSOs Do?

Accountability is not enforcement—and it is not a burden CSOs should carry alone. Civil society cannot replace states, and it cannot be expected to build forensic, legal, or investigative capacities it does not have. But even in severely constrained environments, some choices can reduce harm and preserve options.

The goal is not to "produce accountability." It is to avoid making accountability impossible.

Keep Accountability Minimal But Intentional

For most CSOs, accountability cannot be a function or a strategy. It can, however, be an orientation.

In practice, this means:

- Recognizing that a cyber incident is not only an IT problem, even if IT support is outsourced or nonexistent
- Ensuring that at least one senior decision-maker is aware when an incident occurs
- Accepting that what disappears undocumented disappears permanently—for defense, for learning, and for accountability

This does not require specialized staff. It requires awareness and restraint: do not erase, overwrite, or improvise under pressure if it can be avoided.

(*continued*)

(continued)

Preserve What Already Exists—Do Not Try to Create What You Don't Have

CSOs should not be asked to generate forensic evidence. That is unrealistic.

What is realistic:

- Keeping simple records of what happened, when, and how it was noticed
- Preserving existing logs, emails, screenshots, or messages rather than cleaning systems immediately
- Noting decisions taken under pressure (shutdowns, communications, notifications)

Short, imperfect notes are better than none. Precision matters less than continuity. Accountability often depends on fragments preserved early, not perfect reconstruction later.

Do Not Attempt Accountability Alone, Even Informally

Isolation is one of the strongest advantages attackers have.

CSOs should not seek experts they cannot afford. They should:

- Identify one trusted external point (another CSO, a network, a federation, an intermediary; see the list of experts in Chapter 2) they can inform when something serious happens
- Avoid handling incidents entirely in silence when silent failure carries long-term risk
- Accept that sharing partial information, cautiously and selectively, is often safer than carrying uncertainty alone

Patterns emerge across organizations rather than within one. No single CSO needs the full picture to contribute to it.

Engage Selectively, Not by Default

Engaging authorities, donors, or public attribution processes is not always protective. In many contexts, it can increase exposure.

CSOs should therefore:

- Not feel obliged to report, disclose, or escalate immediately
- Assume that transparency without protection can amplify harm
- Seek advice—even informal—before engaging in public or legal processes

Sometimes the safest choice is delay. Sometimes it is silence. These are not failures; they are survival decisions.

Coordinate Expectations, Not Actions

Most CSOs cannot coordinate responses. That is unrealistic.

What is achievable:

- Aligning messages rather than operations
- Articulating shared risks, recurring failures, and protection gaps through coalitions or umbrella organizations
- Expressing needs collectively, even if responses remain individual

(*continued*)

(*continued*)

Civil society should not be asked to professionalize accountability. It should be enabled to retain agency under constraint.

The burden of investigation, attribution, enforcement, and remedy remains with states. The role of civil society, in realistic terms, is more limited—but still consequential:

- To preserve traces rather than perfection
- To connect rather than isolate
- To choose exposure carefully
- To ensure that harm, once inflicted, cannot be rewritten out of existence

Accountability in cyberspace is not abstract. It determines who bears risk, who absorbs harm, and who escapes consequence. Without accountability, resilience erodes. Without consequence, protection collapses.

Accountability is therefore not an optional complement to digital security—it is the condition that makes security credible, rights enforceable, and resilience sustainable.

How Can We Track Cyberattacks and Information Manipulation Efficiently? Discover the Protect·ngo Cyber Tracer

To address the increasing threat to civil society, Protect·ngo launched the Cyber Tracer. Building on years of expertise in strengthening cyber resilience, we decided to make this platform publicly accessible. It leverages AI to track and analyze cyber incidents targeting CSOs, including malware infections, vulnerabilities, phishing threats, and more. This platform provides policymakers and stakeholders with actionable intelligence and insights to help organizations mitigate risks, and advocates for justice by supplying data that supports accountability efforts.

The Tracer is built with a user-centric approach, ensuring that complex cyber data is presented in a clear and accessible format through intuitive visualizations. The platform also integrates real-world stories from CSOs affected by cyberattacks, reinforcing the urgency of digital resilience.

Updated weekly, the platform empowers users to proactively address emerging threats with timely, actionable insights, while demonstrating the real-world harm of cyberattacks. Developed and maintained by Protect·ngo's cybersecurity experts and software engineers, the Tracer aggregates intelligence from commercial partners, open-source data, and direct reports from affected organizations.

The Tracer stands out through its partnerships with specialist data providers and its integration of AI and large language model (LLM) capabilities. These innovations enhance the platform's ability to deliver data-driven insights into cyber threats, providing a more comprehensive understanding of the risks facing civil society.

The goal of this public review is not to frighten CSO leaders or incite public panic. Information is power. Ignoring these attacks or pretending they don't exist will get us nowhere—we must confront them directly to gauge the scale of the threat and tailor our response. Civil society, the public, and leaders must be aware of the dangers to act as quickly and effectively as possible. That's why our platform is accessible to everyone, in order to popularize this knowledge and make it available to as many people as possible.

(*continued*)

(*continued*)

This will strengthen the fight against cyberattacks targeting CSOs.

The Tracer will continue to evolve: we are actively expanding the platform to include focused areas of interest, such as more location- and sector-specific analysis, and detailed information about the specific harms caused by these cyberattacks (Figure 3.1). This will provide even more granular insight and tailored support to CSOs facing cyber threats.

FIGURE 3.1 Nonprofits per country targeted by cyberattacks.

Source: Protect^{ngo} Cyber Tracer, February 2026

Sources

Artificial Intelligence, Accountability, and Regulation

AoI Action Summit. "Chair's Summary and Political Declaration." Paris, February 2025

Down, Aisha. "AI Firm Claims It Stopped Chinese State-Sponsored Cyber-Attack Campaign." *The Guardian*, November 14, 2025 https://www.theguardian.com/technology/2025/nov/14/ai-anthropic-chinese-state-sponsored-cyber-attack

European Commission. "Artificial Intelligence Act (AI Act)." https://digital-strategy.ec.europa.eu/en/policies/regulatory-framework-ai

Giuffrida, Angela. "Italy First in EU to Pass Comprehensive Law Regulating Use of AI." *The Guardian*, September 18, 2025. https://www.theguardian.com/world/2025/sep/18/italy-first-in-eu-to-pass-comprehensive-law-regulating-ai

International Scientific Report on the Safety of Advanced AI. "The International AI Safety Report." January 2025. https://internationalaioosafetyreport.org/sites/default/files/2025-10/international_ai_safety_report_2025_english.pdf

US Department of Commerce, National Institute of Standards and Technology (NIST). "NIST Identifies Types of Cyberattacks That Manipulate Behavior of AI Systems." January 4, 2024. https://www.nist.gov/news-events/news/2024/01/nist-identifies-types-cyberattacks-manipulate-behavior-ai-systems

Attribution, Accountability, and Cyber Stability

Geneva Centre for Security Sector Governance (DCAF). *Accountability in Cybersecurity*, Edited by Franziska Klopfer. December 2024. https://www.dcaf.ch/sites/default/files/publications/documents/accountability-cyber security.pdf

Pawlak, Patryk. "Accountability in Cyberspace: The Holy Grail of Cyber Stability?" *EU Cyber Direct*, March 2024. https://www.universiteitleiden.nl/binaries/content/assets/governance-and-global-affairs/isga/accountability-in-cyberspace-patryk-pawlak-march-2024.pdf

Protect[ngo]. "Untangling Accountability in Cyberspace." July 21, 2022. https://protect.ngo/news/untangling-accountability-in-cyberspace

Protect[ngo] & The Hague Centre for Strategic Studies. "Cyber Transparency Value Chain: From Awareness and Understanding to Attribution." *Monitoring and Sanctioning*, January 2024. https://hcss.nl/wp-content/uploads/2024/01/Cyber-Transparency-Value-Chain-HCSS-CPI-2024-1.pdf

Harm, Human Impact, and Methodology

Protect[ngo]. *CyberTransparency Value Chain Report, 2024.* Chapters on harm measurement and accountability. https://protect.ngo/resources/cyber-transparency-value-chain

Protect[ngo]. "Harm Methodology: Measuring the Human Impact of Cyberattacks." Ongoing framework, first presented 2023–2024

Cybercrime Ecosystems, Ransomware, and Insurance

Europol. "*Internet Organised Crime Threat Assessment (IOCTA).*" Latest editions, 2023–2024. https://www.europol.europa.eu/iocta

Kaspersky, Eugene. "Un tournant dans la cybersécurité : Une compagnie d'assurance doit verser 1,4 milliards de dollars." February 2, 2022. https://eugene.kaspersky.fr/2022/02/02/un-tournant-dans-la-cybersecurite-une-compagnie-dassurance-doit-verser-une-indemnite-de-14-milliards-de-dollars

United Nations Office on Drugs and Crime (UNODC). *Transnational Organized Crime and the Convergence of Cyber-Enabled Fraud, Underground Banking and Technological Innovation in Southeast Asia.* October 2024. https://www.unodc.org/roseap/uploads/documents/Publications/2024/TOC_Convergence_Report_2024.pdf

Surveillance, Spyware, and State Responsibility

European Council. "Sanctions Against Cyber-Attacks." https://www.consilium.europa.eu/en/policies/sanctions-against-cyber-attacks

European Parliament. "Recommendation of 15 June 2023 following the investigation into the use of Pegasus and equivalent surveillance spyware (2023/2500(RSP))." https://www.europarl.europa.eu/doceo/document/TA-9-2023-06-15_EN.html

Foreign, Commonwealth & Development Office (UK) and Ministry for Europe and Foreign Affairs (France). *Pall Mall Process: Code of Practice for States to Tackle the Proliferation and Irresponsible Use of Commercial Cyber Intrusion Capabilities.* April 4, 2025. https://www.diplomatie.gouv.fr/IMG/pdf/final_pall_mall_process_-_code_of_practice_for_states_eng_-_clean__cle4e7127.pdf

Civil Society Resilience and Ecosystem Responses

Beyond125 Initiative. "CEO Call on Cybersecurity as a Public Interest / Common Good." 2023–2024

Common Good Cyber Fund. "Founding and Pooled-Donor Model Documentation." 2024–2025

Protect·ngo. "Cyber Builders & Protect·ngo Platform Documentation." 2023–2025

Virtual Routes. "Collective Cyber Resilience and Secure Information-Sharing Models for Civil Society." https://virtual-routes.org

Armed Conflict and Cyberspace

Protect·ngo. "Cyber Attacks in Times of Conflict Platforms and Briefings (Ukraine)." 2022–2024

United Nations. *Discussions on Cyber Operations in Armed Conflict, including OEWG and Related UN Processes*

CHAPTER

4

Solutions: A Security Framework Adapted to CSOs

August 2024. The Caux Palace overlooks Lake Geneva. For the second time, I have the privilege of attending this retreat organized by the International Civil Society Centre. The leaders of the biggest CSOs meet up here to discuss strategy. Around the table are Oxfam, Save the Children, YMCA, Civicus. This year, the impact of budget cuts, in particular those coming from the United States, is the main subject. We share the same stories. Colleagues unable to continue their activities, organizations closing down, jobs disappearing, and, behind this collapse, millions of vulnerable people whose situation is only getting worse.

When my turn comes, I talk about increased digital fragility. CSOs, caught in the trap of budget cuts, turn to project financing. But how can they invest in long-term data protection, the responsible use of AI, and cybersecurity governance when they are forced to run from project to project just to make ends meet? It's a perverse mechanism: less money, more competition, less financing, less resilience, more vulnerability.

This fragility issue isn't specific to CSOs. In this regard, CSOs aren't so different from microenterprises and SMEs, or even, in the case of certain global-scale organizations, from multinational corporations. All these entities share the same fundamental needs to ensure their digital resilience. These fundamentals read as the variables of a complex equation: data, AI, cybersecurity, talent, and finances.

Because to think of digital resilience is, more than anything else, to think about data. In order to defend itself from cyberattacks of all kinds, a CSO must have an extremely robust strategy when it comes to data governance. It has to start with these very basic questions: What data do I need in order to operate? Where can I source it? What are the risks associated with that?

Armed with this strategy, the CSO must then think about its choices regarding technology. All these choices will impact the organization's cybersecurity posture—whether they are related to storage, processing, cloud, or (maybe most importantly) AI.

Once CSO leaders have a solid grasp on what's at stake when it comes to their data policy and positioning in terms of AI, that's when they can come up with a cybersecurity strategy. Of course, this kind of strategy doesn't appear in a vacuum. External factors must be considered—which threats are the most prevalent, whether the organization's actions are exposed to geopolitical tensions that might escalate into cyberattacks—but at the end of the day, when we have a clear vision of our data and technology, we can consider cybersecurity in an informed and rational manner. I'm describing these steps in an incremental way with clear pedagogical intentions. These decisions regarding data, AI, and cybersecurity are generally made together, within a broader digital resilience plan. This must be undertaken with humility: digital resilience plans usually don't last long when confronted with reality, starting with available human resources and, in the case of CSOs, with fundraising.

Available cybersecurity talent is the great weakness of civil society. I've mentioned it time and time again in this book. As for the financial aspect, the sector is facing a major crisis. Not only are funds increasingly low, but traditional fundraising mechanisms are no longer relevant. We were reminded of these issues by the international civil society CEO call in 2024 (see the sources at the end of this chapter).

So, what can be done? This chapter is all about solutions, and if you are curious, check the number of pages you have left to read: you will understand that many options exist. That's civil society's prerogative. Resilience is central to its mission, and it has adapted to this lack of talent and budget. This chapter lists solutions built by civil society for civil society. We will go through each of them, following the National Institute of Standards and Technology (NIST) Cybersecurity Framework and adapting it to the specific needs of CSOs. Many organizations or initiatives rooted in civil society are active in the categories present in the NIST framework—identification, protection, detection, response following an incident, and recovery after an attack. Some of them focus on a single one of these steps, in a vertical approach; others offer a more holistic service. In order to build on this framework, I will introduce two complementary dimensions: creating and facilitating access to cybersecurity talent, and making funds available.

Adapting the NIST Framework to CSOs

The NIST Cybersecurity Framework (CSF) is a globally recognized model designed to help organizations understand, manage, and reduce cybersecurity risks. Originally created by the U.S.

National Institute of Standards and Technology for critical infrastructure, it has since evolved into a flexible, sector-agnostic framework used by governments, enterprises, small businesses, and, increasingly, nonprofits. Recent updates, such as NIST CSF 2.0, explicitly broaden its applicability to organizations "from the smallest schools and nonprofits to the largest agencies and corporations," highlighting its universal relevance.

At its core, the NIST CSF is structured around five essential functions: Identify, Protect, Detect, Respond, and Recover (Figure 4.1). These provide a coherent lifecycle for cybersecurity readiness. For CSOs, these functions form a practical blueprint for resilience. I propose here an augmented version of NIST for CSOs, adding Enable and Empower, which are critical for civil society.

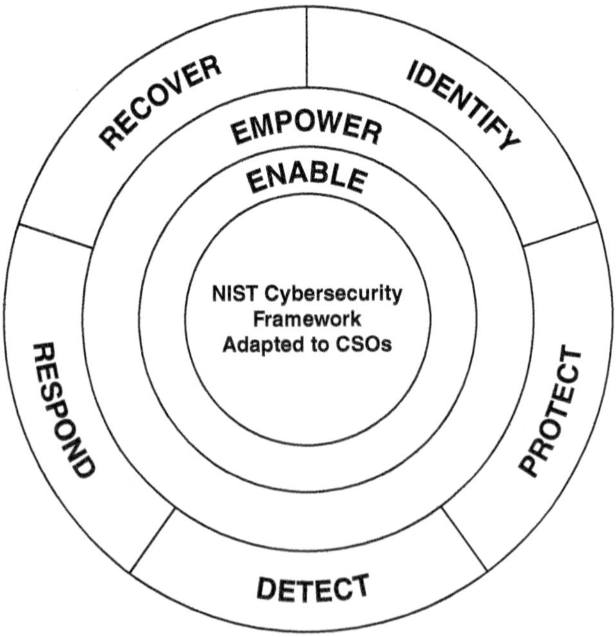

FIGURE 4.1 NIST Cybersecurity Framework Adapted to CSOs.

Source: Protect.ngo, 2026

Identify is the foundation. It focuses on understanding assets, risks, and governance structures. Research on CSO cyber maturity shows that many organizations still struggle at this stage, with significant gaps in areas such as asset management and risk assessment. Without clarity on what needs protection—data, systems, operations—CSOs cannot effectively advance toward security. Internal assessments such as the Protect·ngo General Cyber Security Assessment help nonprofits evaluate their maturity using the NIST framework through accessible, nontechnical tools.

Protect covers safeguards like access control, training, and secure configuration. CSOs often rely on mixed technology environments, volunteer contributors, and external partners, making protective measures essential yet challenging. Capacity-building initiatives, such as cyber volunteer networks (see Builders below) or cybersecurity clinics, help fill these gaps by providing expert support to CSOs that lack skilled cybersecurity personnel.

Detect focuses on timely discovery of cybersecurity events. AI-powered threat-intelligence services tailored to nonprofits allow for early identification of vulnerabilities, data leaks, and targeted attacks against CSOs. For CSOs working in sensitive humanitarian or political contexts, such detection capabilities are crucial. Examples of this include the data feeds provided by The Shadowserver Foundation, the Cyber Threat Alliance, and the Tracer.

Respond ensures that once an incident is detected, the organization can contain and mitigate it. Although many CSOs lack formal incident response teams, the NIST framework provides structured guidance to develop lightweight, context-appropriate response plans. Community-based secure information-sharing platforms, such as FIRST, the NGO-ISAC, the NetHope services, or the UnderServed project, further strengthen response capabilities by helping NGOs learn from each other's experiences.

Recover focuses on restoring normal operations and learning from incidents. For organizations delivering essential services, downtime can directly impact communities in need. NIST's emphasis on resilience, documentation, and continuous improvement helps CSOs institutionalize recovery processes that were previously ad hoc or undocumented. This is where initiatives like the Builders or NetHope also come into play.

In an expanded version of the framework, an additional function—Empower—recognizes that cybersecurity maturity in CSOs depends on people as much as technology. Many nonprofits lack in-house cyber expertise, rely heavily on volunteers, or struggle to attract and retain skilled staff in competitive markets. The Empower function expands access to critical talent through volunteer networks, shared-services models, fellowships, and public-private partnerships. It helps organizations map needed competencies, build internal learning pathways, and integrate external expert support where required. By institutionalizing the development and provisioning of talent, this function ensures CSOs not only react to risks but also build the human capital necessary to anticipate, manage, and shape their cybersecurity posture strategically.

Another function I will add to address the specific needs of civil society—Enable—tackles the structural challenge many CSOs face: securing the financial resources needed to build long-term organizational resilience. While the traditional NIST functions help CSOs assess and manage technical risk, they do not directly address the chronic underfunding of cybersecurity capacity in civil society. The Enable function drives the development of sustainable financing models for organizational development, including cybersecurity investments, digital infrastructure, and capacity-building programs. It guides CSOs in structuring multiyear resource plans, diversifying funding sources, and engaging donors in viewing digital risk as a core element of mission delivery. By embedding financial sustainability into the cybersecurity lifecycle, CSOs strengthen their ability to maintain security controls, retain expertise, and evolve their defenses as threats increase. Initiatives such as the Common Good Cyber Fund or the FAGI in Geneva fit into this category.

Beyond this lifecycle, the NIST framework's greatest value for CSOs may lie in its adaptability. CSOs are not fundamentally different from for-profit organizations regarding the need for strong data governance, technology choices, and long-term resilience. Such a framework helps CSOs operationalize a global action plan, such as the Beyond125 action plan launched in the City of The Hague, and cyber maturity assessments based on the NIST framework have already helped hundreds of nonprofits benchmark their security posture and progress over time. In an environment where cyber threats increasingly target civil society, the NIST CSF provides CSOs with a structured, accessible, and globally validated path toward security—not as a rigid standard, but as a practical roadmap tailored to their mission-driven realities.

Empower: Anticipating, Managing, and Expanding

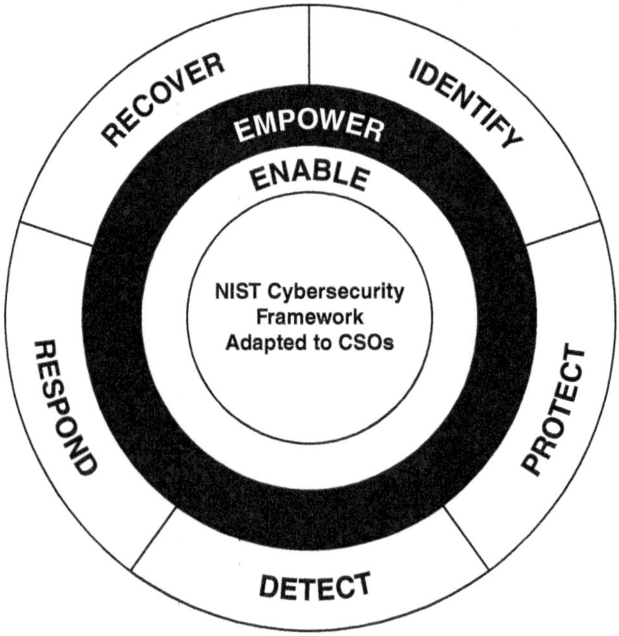

The Empower function recognizes that people—not just tools—drive cybersecurity maturity in CSOs. It focuses on expanding access to expertise through volunteer networks, shared services, fellowships, and internal capacity-building. By strengthening human capital, CSOs develop the skills and confidence needed to anticipate and manage digital risks strategically. Strong leaders dedicated to this function are the Builders and the Cyber Resilience Corps, both of which act as parts of a global plan for CSO resilience, Beyond125.

Helping in Our Own Way: The Cyber Builders Program

The Basics: What Is the Builders Program? The Builders, or Cyber Builders, is our community made up of cybersecurity experts, companies, researchers, volunteers, funders, and partners who come together in collaboration to build collective resilience. We encourage participants to exchange and share tips, advice, and warnings, notify each other about risks, and learn best practices. Community is vital when it comes to protecting the most vulnerable. Joining forces gives each of us a fighting chance when facing cyber threats.

In addition to this community aspect, at the heart of the Builders is a program that links CSOs that need cybersecurity assistance with volunteers who are ready to guide them free of charge. It exists as a bridge between organizations in need and professionals who have the knowledge and resources necessary to help them out.

On one side, CSOs that become aware of their poor digital resilience contact us to ask for help. This service is entirely free, since the goal of the Builders, among other things, is to offer a solution to compensate for organizations' insufficient budget. In order to enter the program, the organization must be recognized as a nonprofit entity, volunteer group, or institution carrying a social mission, and must be nongovernmental. It must also work in favor of supporting vulnerable individuals or communities, in whatever sector it may be (health, education, hunger. . .). The program welcomes CSOs from around the world, whether their reach is local, national, or international. Sometimes, we are contacted not by organizations themselves, but by philanthropic foundations that provide financial support to various civil society actors. This way, foundations can protect their grantees or beneficiaries by strengthening their own digital defenses, but also obtain help for the various CSOs they support.

> The challenges of cybersecurity cut across every strand of modern civil society. We cannot leave anyone behind, because none of us can be adequately secure until we have helped everyone else around us shore up their defenses.
>
> —Hani Banayoti, Builder

On the other side, opposite civil society, we have volunteers, who we nickname Builders. The program depends entirely on their commitment and generosity. They are professionals employed by private companies, with at least one year of experience in cybersecurity. These are people who understand the importance of sharing information and the necessity of protecting civil society, and who decide to act in favor of this by donating their time and leveraging their skills. Some give one to two hours a month; others do more. Any mission, any contact made with a CSO matters and can help prevent a future cyberattack, or at least limit its damage. As for us, we stand behind them, coordinating the program and offering our support by sharing resources and tips so they feel confident about the training they provide. Some Builders sign up individually and of their own accord. But sometimes, companies also join the program, thus becoming our commercial partners, and encourage their qualified employees to donate their time through us.

> We did not know who to turn to for professional help until we learned about the services provided by Protect·ngo. Their staff were extremely responsive. They took all our concerns seriously and helped us check several technical details. They were holding our hand as we found our way through the crisis. Having someone available to advise us was invaluable in what for us was a previously unknown situation.
>
> Once the crisis was over, Protect·ngo continued to provide support through its volunteering program, the Builders, which bridges experts in cybersecurity with humanitarian

> NGOs. The Builders carried out an audit of our system and helped us develop a response plan.
>
> Since then, we have been receiving help to strengthen staff awareness and improve our settings and general practices. Receiving such hands-on technical help has allowed us to implement additional security measures that we didn't know existed. We have learned a lot in a very short period of time and feel much better equipped to operate in a changing workspace where there are real online risks.
>
> —Christina WILLE, Director of Insecurity Insight

How Does It Work Exactly? When a CSO contacts us and expresses its fears, we start by assessing its digital resilience. This is done through a questionnaire that addresses subjects linked to cybersecurity in a very broad way. Following this assessment, the organization can be fully integrated into the program through the dedicated platform (Figure 4.2), and we steer them toward appropriate actions.

The program is made up of missions. Each mission has a particular theme: backup advice, AI skills training, cloud services mapping, incident response plan review, and so on. In its personal space, the nonprofit can select the missions it is interested in. Then, on the Builders' side of the platform, pending missions appear and volunteers can be put in contact with the organization that made the request.

FIGURE 4.2 The Builders platform.

Source: Cyber Builders, Protect·ngo, 2026

> The Builder did an exceptional job creating a highly realistic phishing email. By exposing our team to this exercise, we gained a deep understanding of our vulnerabilities and the potential risks we face. This exercise highlighted the need for ongoing cybersecurity awareness. We will be providing training to all staff later this week. We are genuinely grateful to the Builders for making this happen.
>
> —Anonymous

Each mission lasts between one and four hours, depending on its complexity. Based on the nature of the mission, the Builder shares theoretical knowledge, tools, and resources, or creates a practical exercise or simulation. This is the case, for example, for phishing exercises (see text box above). Most missions require at least one video call with the CSO, but the communication channels can be flexible. For example, in the case of dark web monitoring, consisting of research to determine if information relative to the nonprofit has leaked, if the Builder finds no compromised data, a written report can suffice. Volunteers can accept certain missions depending on their availability and willingness to discuss directly with the CSO. At the end of a mission, the nonprofit as well as the Builder give us feedback so that we can ensure the program is functioning as it should.

In addition to the missions, the CSOs' personal space on the Builders platform grants them access to complementary services. First off, a personal dashboard shows them the score they got on the initial assessment, the missions completed and those still pending, and a few other useful figures. Another page allows them to follow, in real time, the number of credentials belonging to members of their organization that have leaked on the Web, as well as vulnerabilities detected in their system. They can also go through profiles of cybersecurity professionals looking for employment, in case they would like to hire an expert internally for more thorough support. And finally, through the platform, they have access to a digital library containing a large collection of resources.

The Builders program aims to equip CSOs with knowledge, resources, and practical tools to strengthen their long-term protection, in the hope that they will become as autonomous as possible when it comes to their resilience. It represents a first step toward real collaboration between the private and public sectors. Our volunteers, the Builders, know how to share their knowledge in a way that allows robust defense to be implemented quickly. It's a program built on solidarity and the collective wish to help CSOs and protect the most vulnerable.

> [The Builder] has been great in guiding us on where to start with our journey on the implementation of enrolling devices to Intune as a way of being able to control where our Microsoft accounts are being set up and used. We are beginners in this expertise and didn't know where to start, but [the Builder] has definitely helped us identify where to start and tackle different scenarios of enrolling devices in our organization. Thank you [Builder]!
>
> —Fondation suisse de déminage

To this day, the Builders program has accumulated 3,829 hours of volunteering divided between its 1,592 Builders. Forty-eight companies have joined us as commercial partners. Thanks to all this, we have been able to help 655 CSOs in total. The impacts of this mobilization are far-reaching, but our ambition is greater, and we will continue to develop the program to make civil society stronger worldwide.

Who Benefits from the Builders?

Civil Society Organizations and Charitable Foundations The initial goal of the Builders is simple: help CSOs support each other and provide them with free external support when needed, and that's the main advantage they gain from participating in the program. But let's dig a bit deeper into what that means, and we will see that strong digital resilience has many indirect benefits.

Because each nonprofit is different, the advice and training they receive are personalized as much as possible. They discuss their situation with the Builders who assist them, and missions can be adapted to the specific needs of each organization. They benefit from tailor-made support provided by attentive professionals.

> The support provided by Protect.ngo has been invaluable to SOS Children's Villages International. Its expert review of our Global Cybersecurity Regulation, along with a standardized cybersecurity assessment, significantly strengthened our security posture.
>
> —SOS Children's Villages

Efficient protection against cyberattacks leads to stronger trust from donors and beneficiaries toward the organization. It's important for CSOs to show them that they are serious about protecting their donations and personal information, and that they act accordingly. Even though an unexpected attack is always a possibility if criminals detect a vulnerability the nonprofit is unaware of, by investing in their cybersecurity, they show knowledge of the dangers and willingness to address them—and that's often what matters most to donors.

The Builders isn't just a program: it's a community, building itself brick by brick around common values. By joining us, CSOs can get to know one another and share their practices in order to build collective resilience, which, in the long term, will be beneficial to civil society as a whole.

> The missions offered by the Builders have been incredibly helpful, and the new mission tab on the website offers a more structured overview of our progress. Protect.ngo is a crucial partner for discussing important cybersecurity issues and providing consultancy.
>
> —Handicap International

Cyber volunteers Volunteering in general is, before anything else, a way to give a bit of oneself in order to help others; but volunteers also gain something valuable. Most of our Builders feel great satisfaction when they can leverage their skills to help civil society. That way, in addition to their job in the private sector, they find a way to pitch in for issues that matter to them. Knowing that human beings from underprivileged or vulnerable populations depend on their work is deeply rewarding and fosters a sense of community.

> I've been volunteering with [the Builders] for more than a year, being one of the top 3 volunteers over 2024. I highly value [their] work helping NGOs become more secure in a global cyber landscape. I like the plethora of missions and organizations on the platform and how engaged the Protect.ngo team is coordinating the efforts. The different missions allow me to explore different areas of cybersecurity and keep my skillset sharp while helping others. The global nature of the work being done, as well as the connection of the Builders, gives me a sense of purpose and community that I highly value in my life!
>
> —Panagiotis Vlachos, Builder

It's also a learning opportunity for volunteers. Through their engagement in the program, Builders can maintain their existing skills and acquire new ones. In the civil society sector, cybersecurity isn't applied in the exact same way, or with the same stakes, as in the private industry. This practice allows the Builders to understand how their area of expertise can be applied to a new context. It's also important to note that in the computer systems and technology sectors, progress is quick, and it isn't possible to keep an eye on all the advancements. Each employee, each volunteer has their own set of specializations. Builders can collaborate on missions when multiple areas of expertise are necessary. By working together, they can learn from one another and acquire new skills that their private-sector job might not have provided.

> I'm grateful for the opportunity to collaborate with Protect^{ngo}, whose dedication to creating a safer digital world inspires me every day. Let's continue to push the boundaries of what's possible in cybersecurity and create a more secure digital environment for everyone.
>
> —Melanie Hendrickx, Builder

In the same way that the program builds an international community of CSOs, it creates connections between volunteers worldwide. They have the opportunity to exchange ideas, and even meet in person during the events we organize, sometimes independently, sometimes in partnership with other volunteer communities, like the Cyber Resilience Corps in the United States (see the next section). These events have become a hub for exchanging ideas, and they give volunteers the chance to discuss practices and build the future of cyber volunteering.

> With over a decade of experience working in the nonprofit sector, I understand cybersecurity challenges at their core. Volunteering with the Builders allows me to turn that understanding into action, helping organizations protect their missions and the people they serve.
>
> —Abdulkadir M. Nurein, Builder

Private Companies Private-sector companies must take on part of the responsibility so that together, we can achieve peace in cyberspace. Investing in programs like the Builders is part of this effort. When a company joins us, that represents dozens of potential new Builders, and a commercial partner that provides stability to the initiative so that we can further our mission. But the company itself benefits from it as well.

By joining the Builders, companies strengthen their image in terms of social responsibility. Showcasing that kind of partnership is beneficial to a company's reputation. It also generates real social impact, which attracts clients and new partners, as well as talent who want to work for a socially conscious company.

Participating in projects such as the Builders also positions the company as a headliner when it comes to cybersecurity. It shows adaptability to technological advancements and a real awareness of what's at stake, and also attracts clients, partners, and talent. This factor can come into play when a company is being compared to its competition in any context.

Finally, the community aspect is also important for companies. By joining a network of organizations, foundations, and companies that share the same human values, they can help civil society work toward a safer cyberspace, but also position themselves strategically in the market.

Zooming Out: What Comes Next? 2025 was a year of important developments in the Builders program, with the start of local chapters. Their objective is to create communities on a local level. Each is led by an experienced Builder, who coordinates the chapter to foster collaboration between local volunteers. We encourage them to meet up and exchange regularly, share their respective experiences and practices, collaborate on missions, and build a solid community based on common values.

Chapters have already been opened in New York, Geneva, Dublin, and The Hague, and it's only the beginning. We are lucky to have among us Builders who are motivated to take on more responsibilities within the program and lead their peers and all of civil society toward a more secure future. We have the ambition of helping 1 million CSOs by 2035, and this goal would be unrealizable without the Builders' commitment.

I like to volunteer in this program because it gives me an opportunity to work with people who are making this world a better place to live. I have a very good time working with NGOs in this program and sometimes, yes, we do run into challenges because of the number of pieces involved and the number of people who are involved in making decisions. However, once we have the plan, it makes our job easy and that also brings a huge change in their organization. This is an amazing initiative because I have seen organizations make huge differences in their workplace to make it more secure. And once they have those measures in place and their workplace is more secure, they can focus more on the work that they want to do.

—Minu Singa, Builder

Learn More About the Builders

We would be thrilled to have you among us and to help you anywaywecan.Tojoinus,pleasevisitwww`.protect.ngo/the-builders`.

Get help as a CSO: `https://protect.ngo/act-now/nonprofit`

Start volunteering: `https://protect.ngo/act-now/volunteer`

Sign up as a foundation: `https://protect.ngo/act-now/foundation`

Sign up as a company: `https://protect.ngo/act-now/corporation`

Cyber Resilience Corps

What Is It and How Does It Work? The Cyber Resilience Corps (CRC) is an initiative that relies on cyber volunteering, just like the Builders program. It also originated from Protect·ngo, in partnership with UC Berkeley's Center for Long-Term Cybersecurity (CLTC) in San Francisco. This collaboration is very important to us because we share many common values with the CLTC—its mission is to make access to cybersecurity available to everyone, and it works on multiple fronts at once to help us adapt collectively to the challenges of the digital world.

By starting the Cyber Resilience Corps, our common goal was to defend institutions that drive society forward. The CRC is present all over the United States and brings assistance to civil society, but also to hospitals, schools, municipalities, and small businesses (Figure 4.3). The United States being among the most frequently targeted countries in terms of cyberattacks, we hope the CRC can lead them toward a more resilient future in cyberspace, for the good of all the communities who live there or depend on them.

The difference between the CRC and the Builders is that this isn't the first initiative in the United States focusing on

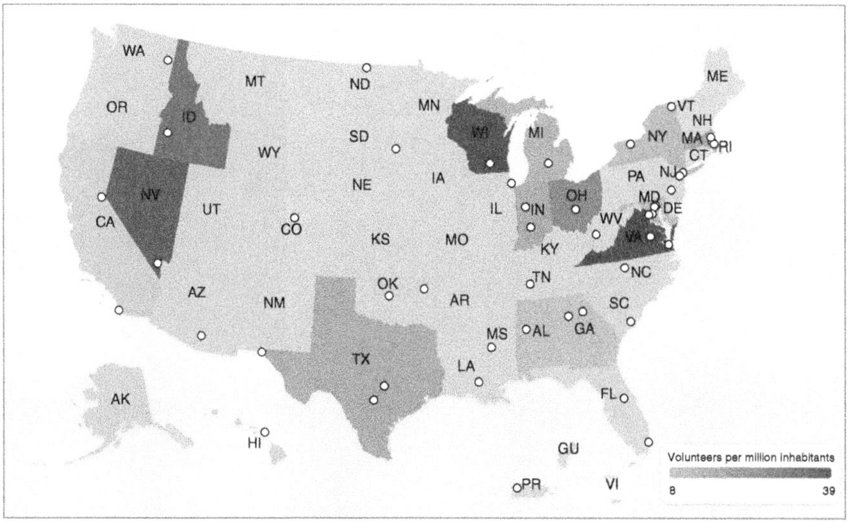

FIGURE 4.3 CRC volunteers by U.S. state.

Source: Cyber Resilience Corps, 2026

matching CSOs with cybersecurity experts. There are a few existing volunteer networks offering their help to civil society; the work they do is essential and they sometimes suffer from lack of visibility. The objective of the CRC is absolutely not to create competition, which could harm existing structures; instead, it has taken on a role more akin to strategic coordination, expansion, and reinforcement of existing initiatives.

Institutions wishing to receive cybersecurity support are able to quickly access the list of CRC-certified volunteer networks operating in their area and that are able to cater to their specific needs. They can view basic information on these networks (region, services, number of volunteers, and missions completed) and can then contact them directly if they choose to. This coordination service is free of charge.

Individuals who wish to donate their time and leverage their skills to help these institutions can also find volunteer networks that they can join, depending on their situation. This service is free as well. Volunteers come from all over the world, as most missions are easily achievable remotely.

> We are looking forward to the next couple of years, which will see tremendous growth in volunteer coordination. There are many people working in cybersecurity in the United States, but very few understand that they can lend a small portion of their time to protect their communities and public-interest institutions that protect us all in return. We keep hearing, "we want to help, we just don't know how." Getting involved with the Cyber Resilience Corps provides the avenue for them to do just that.
>
> —Jessica Walton, US Regional Officer, Protect$^{\cdot ngo}$

Who Benefits from It?

Supported Institutions Institutions participating in the program, all based in the United States, are put in contact directly with networks of volunteers who are able to cater to their needs and help them strengthen their digital resilience. For them, it's an opportunity to learn more about cybersecurity, to set up defenses, and to train their leaders, volunteers, and employees efficiently. This service can have a huge impact on institutions that commit.

CSOs are not the only structures that can benefit from the Cyber Resilience Corps' support. The service is also offered to entities from the public sector (state, local, territorial, or tribal governments; schools, hospitals, municipal agencies, etc.) and from the private sector (small and medium businesses, particularly those providing essential services, for example clinics and supply chain providers). The CRC welcomes institutions operating in over 20 areas: development, education, environment, human rights, peace, justice, and more.

In practical terms, the institutions that join the CRC benefit from a cybersecurity strategy assessment, support as they implement new tools, training for their members, assistance in incident response, and monitoring of their networks to help them identify potential threats.

Cyber volunteers As previously mentioned, many private-sector employees are eager to donate time and leverage their expertise to the benefit of CSOs and other institutions that are particularly vulnerable in cyberspace. Cyber volunteering is their chance to use and perfect their skills, to generate real social and human impact, and to enter a network of volunteers who share their values.

At the Cyber Resilience Corps, volunteers can be current or former employees of the private and public sectors, but also students and retirees, as long as their desires and skills are compatible with at least one type of mission covered by the various partner volunteer networks. For those who already volunteer in one of these existing networks, entering the CRC program through their network leads to greater visibility, more missions, and heightened social impact.

Lastly, the CRC allows for connection between volunteers, whether they are employees, students, or retirees. In December 2025, the first Cyber Volunteering Day took place—a day full of encounters and exchanges: best practices, advice, tips, and networking. It was an opportunity for cyber volunteers to meet people whose roads they probably wouldn't have crossed in any other context, and to witness the expansion of the network, which has flourished into a vibrant community.

> Cyber Volunteer Day was a very practical and useful collaborative exercise. It brought together numerous organizations, including state cyber emergency response teams, community emergency response teams (CERT), university cyber clinics, cyber insurers, and nonprofits involved in cyber volunteer efforts. These initiatives will grow in importance and hopefully expand in the years to come. It's imperative that we better insulate small organizations from cyberattacks through ongoing coordination at multiple levels.
>
> —Mark Schreiber, Cyber Volunteer Day participant

Learn More About the Cyber Resilience Corps

Interested in this initiative? For more information, please visit `https://www.cybervolunteers.us/en`.

Get help: `https://www.cybervolunteers.us/en#for-organizations`

Start volunteering: `https://www.cybervolunteers.us/en#for-volunteers`

Make a donation: `https://www.cybervolunteers.us/en/donate`

Beyond125 (The Hague, 2024)

Beyond125 is a project born in The Hague, in collaboration with the Paris Peace Forum, the Global Forum on Cyber Expertise, and The Hague Humanity Hub. It follows the call from civil society leaders for better protection online and is presented as a four-step action plan to bring hands-on solutions for CSOs' cybersecurity gap (Figure 4.4).

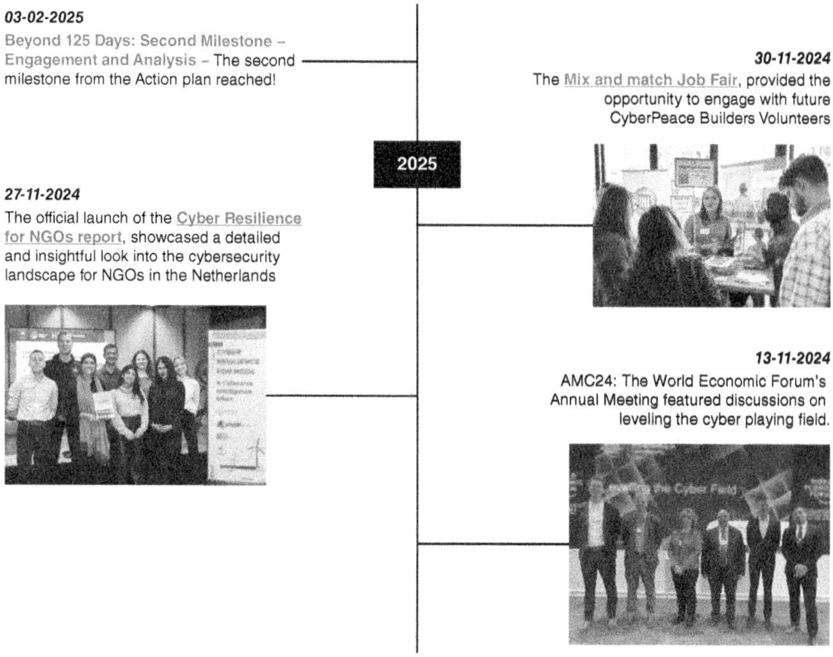

FIGURE 4.4 Beyond125's four-step action plan.

Source: Beyond125, 2026

The first step of this plan, executed immediately after the launch of Beyond125, was sharing information and raising awareness about the great vulnerability of civil society. The second step consisted of publicly documenting the harm caused by cyberattacks to nonprofits all over the world. This work led to the publication of various reports, focusing, among other topics, on collective resilience, nonprofits of International Geneva, and information manipulation. The third step is dedicated to publishing recommendations that could be useful in supporting CSOs. The fourth and final step is about offering free support centered around AI and cybersecurity to 10,000 CSOs. That's when cyber volunteering programs make their appearance, as they will help us reach this goal.

Learn More About Beyond125

Interested in this initiative? For more information, please visit https://www.beyond125.org.

Reports:

- *A Futures Approach to Tackling Mis-, Dis-, and Malinformation*: https://icscentre.org/knowledge-hub/mis-dis-and-malinformation
- *CyberCAN: Cybersecurity for Cities and Nonprofits*: https://cltc.berkeley.edu/program/cybercan
- *Cyber Resilience for NGOs: A Collective Intelligence Effort*: https://protect.ngo/resources/cyber-resilience-ngos-collective-intelligence-effort
- *Cyber Threats to NGOs*: https://www.cyberthreatalliance.org/resources/assets/cyber-threats-to-ngos
- *From Vulnerability to Resilience: Cybersecurity Challenges for MSMEs in the APAC Region*: https://protect.ngo/resources/cybersecurity-challenges-for-msmes-in-the-apac-region
- *NGOs Serving Humanity at Risk: Cyber Threats Affecting "International Geneva"*: https://geneva.protect.ngo
- *Redefining the Digital Future for Nonprofits*: https://nethope.org/articles/redefining-the-digital-future-nonprofits-on-the-brink-of-a-new-era

Paris Peace Forum: https://parispeaceforum.org

Global Forum on Cyber Expertise (GFCE): `https://thegfce.org`

The Hague Humanity Hub: `https://www.humanityhub.org`

PERSPECTIVE: Cyber Civil Society—UC Berkeley Center for Long-Term Cybersecurity

Community organizations—including nonprofits, hospitals, schools, local utilities, city governments, and small businesses—deliver vital services to the public, but they are often the least prepared to protect themselves or recover from cyberattacks. These organizations are sometimes described as "below the cyber poverty line," because they lack the resources and/or expertise to implement robust cybersecurity programs. Cyberattacks on these organizations put everyone at risk and can lead to the shuttering of critical services. Community organizations are also highly interdependent; just as hospitals need water, small businesses need childcare, and utilities need city governments, which in turn need nonprofits. A cyberattack on one organization has ripple effects across the community.

Despite widely available, free-to-use cybersecurity frameworks, guidebooks, toolkits, and software geared toward community organizations, little progress has been made to shore up community cybersecurity. A "last mile" problem persists: without cyber-proficient expertise on staff, community organizations struggle to translate free resources and fit them to their specific circumstances and threat models. We surveyed nonprofits in the Bay Area and found that 53% of respondents had no full-time IT staff, and those that did had an average of one IT staff member

(*continued*)

(*continued*)

for every 96 employees. Therefore, most cannot deploy or use sophisticated defensive tools even when cybersecurity companies provide them at low or no cost. Trust relationships are also essential to successful engagement with cybersecurity, and many community serving organizations lack preexisting cyber or IT partnerships, and some distrust big tech. Trusted, hands-on cybersecurity support is required for most community-serving organizations to bridge the last mile to community cyber resilience.

The good news is that much of the basic cyber hygiene that community organizations struggle with (patching, identity management, MFA, incident response planning) can be delivered by trained cyber volunteers and has an outsized impact on defending against and recovering from cyberattacks.

We developed the Roadmap to Community Cyber Defense in order to outline a pathway for scaling up community cybersecurity defense.

The roadmap begins with expanding cyber volunteering through programs like university-based cybersecurity clinics, state-based civilian cyber corps, and corporate volunteering.

Next, we need to create shared services, such as Security Operations Centers and Managed Security Services Providers, that provide persistent cybersecurity support to community organizations at below-market cost, using the latest defensive tools.

Third, we must connect volunteers, shared services, and other government-provided resources into long-term support systems by developing regional ecosystems and "connective tissue" among providers.

Finally, we need to embed cyber knowledge in communities, so that organizations' understanding of their role and their own agency in cybersecurity continues to advance.

The roadmap is already underway. National and international networks of hands-on assistance at scale exist via the Cyber Resilience Corps, the Consortium of Cybersecurity Clinics, the Builders, and other programs. These programs overcome the "last mile" barriers to cybersecurity by earning trust in their communities and developing specialized expertise in translating technical digital-risk topics to nontechnical audiences. These programs work because they invest in distributed leadership and local relationships. These programs are growing, but we need to multiply them to reach every community. The threat landscape will continue to evolve, but human networks will remain the essential infrastructure to disseminate fixes.

—Ann Cleaveland, Executive Director of
UC Berkeley Center for Long-Term Cybersecurity

The Center for Long-Term Cybersecurity focuses on bringing practical solutions for cyber resilience to communities everywhere in the United States. A partner of Protect.ngo, it is active in cyber volunteer networks and cybersecurity clinics, and it works to bring resources and education to those who need them.

PERSPECTIVE: Cyber Civil Society—International Civil Society Centre

Here's a confession: last year I was caught two times by a professional phishing attack. One of those was staged by our own operations department in order to keep us alert about cyber threats. One was real and caused financial harm—not to an existential level, but it hurt us financially to clean our IT infrastructure from the virus that was implanted. And

(*continued*)

(*continued*)

despite the general awareness that we all seem to have about these threats—hands up, who has not had similar experiences over the past years?

The rather abstract numbers of cyberattacks on the nonprofit sector are scary enough, as Stéphane Duguin from Protect-ngo outlines in his recent blog article [see Sources]. They become more threatening when you experience them directly, or with peers in partner organizations, and no one can ignore anymore that those threats are real and can be incredibly harmful. We know that the increasing numbers of attacks come with different motives: extortion and blackmail, the desire to harm others, and the simple ability to cause mayhem because it has become so easy. And of course, the most concerning development is linked to the current political climate of rising authoritarianism: countless misinformation, disinformation, and smear campaigns against CSOs, and efforts to polarize societies by extremist actors all over the world.

CSOs have always had an important watchdog function: they stand for global values of solidarity, inclusion, and concern for marginalized groups, and are therefore a potential hindrance to a new world order that seems to be reverting to the power of the strongest and the boldest. We fight for global justice and good governance, which makes us inconvenient for economic and political power holders. And with the rapidly shrinking operating space for civil society, cyberattacks are an accelerating factor reducing our political and social impact.

The World Economic Forum (WEF), in its global risk report, has named misinformation and disinformation, cyber insecurity, and adverse outcomes of AI among the top risks by severity, both short- and long-term, as a constant feature over the past years. These features have strong links to "online harms" and to increasing censorship and surveillance. While the WEF still subsumes these risks under "technological risks," one should acknowledge that we are dealing with sociopolitical developments that threaten the stability of societies and of a liberal and democratic political order, particularly through the active targeting of media, CSOs, and other corrective institutions.

Leaders in civil society who are concerned about justice, inclusion, and equality should therefore make these developments an organizational priority concern and take them out of the "technology" and "IT" niche. We are dealing with a tectonic shift that threatens the very basis upon which our work is grounded. If you look for guidance, the Center has published a document that supports cybersecurity strategies for ICSOs and another one that deals with navigating responses to anti-rights actors.

—Wolfgang Jamann, Executive Director, International Civil Society Centre

The International Civil Society Centre brings together civil society actors to work on some of the most pressing issues of the day. Its mission is to support organizations and bring them long-term resilience and efficiency for the protection of their beneficiaries.

Enable: Securing Resources and Building Capacity

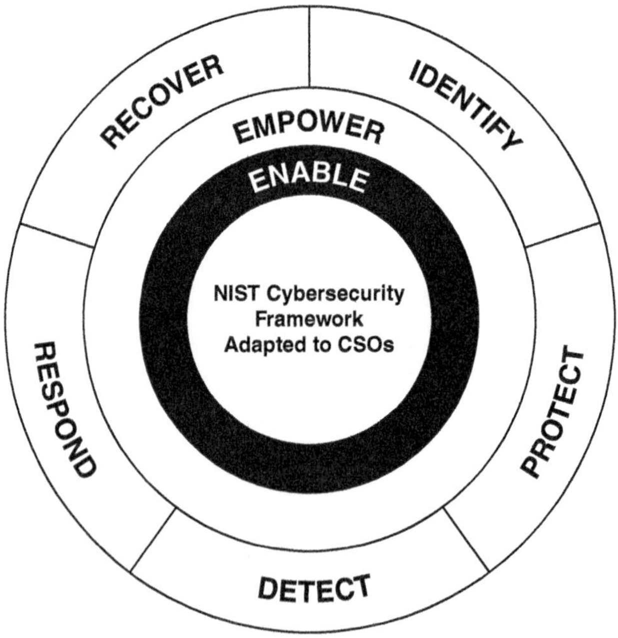

The Enable function addresses the structural challenge of securing long-term resources for cybersecurity in CSOs. It guides organizations in building sustainable funding models, engaging donors, and planning multiyear investments in digital resilience. By embedding financial sustainability into the security lifecycle, CSOs gain the stability needed to maintain and evolve their defenses. Common Good Cyber and the fund it has put in place are an example of how necessary resources can be brought to CSOs.

Common Good Cyber

What Is It and How Does It Work? Common Good Cyber (CGC) is an initiative started by various CSOs dedicated to peace in cyberspace: the Global Cyber Alliance, the Cyber Threat

Alliance, Protect·ngo, FIRST, the Global Forum on Cyber Expertise, the Institute for Security and Technology, and The Shadowserver Foundation. These CSOs have decided to align on this initiative in an effort to face threats together and join forces for their common goal: ensure online safety for all, and particularly for the most vulnerable. They aim to promote collaboration and the funding of institutions and individuals who work behind the scenes to make the Internet a place of safety, built on a strong and healthy foundation.

Since Common Good Cyber was created, member CSOs have come together to think of solutions to strengthen their means and heighten their chances of achieving their goals. An important step was taken in June 2025, when CGC, in partnership with the Internet Society, launched the Common Good Cyber Fund. As soon as this fund was created, the United Kingdom and Canada had already participated in the form of USD 5.7 million; a month later, Australia joined in. This fund will allow CGC to transform its vision into support thanks to resources and hands-on strategies. It will be used to secure central digital infrastructure for the public good, and to provide cybersecurity assistance to those who need it.

Common Good Cyber and Protect·ngo have also designed Beyond125, a four-step action plan and a big step forward. Thanks to this plan, we can take real-life, realistic measures to reinforce civil society's security.

Who Benefits from It? The cybersecurity CSOs that launched Common Good Cyber did so in order to create a platform that would amplify their voices, bring awareness to the public, donors, and states about their cause, and further their mission. They are the direct beneficiaries of the actions undertaken by CGC.

But behind them stand hundreds of nonprofits that rely on them for protection. If CGC receives adequate support and funding, these cybersecurity CSOs can extend their expertise to many other nonprofits, help them train their staff, and respond responsibly to attacks.

What's more, behind these nonprofits, we have millions of individuals whose well-being, dignity, and survival depend on their programs. If CGC accomplishes its mission, the impact will be immense. It will have repercussions across all sectors of civil society and ensure a higher quality of life for communities around the world. It's what I've been saying since the very first pages of this book: we must never lose sight of our ultimate objective—human impact.

Learn More About Common Good Cyber

Interested in this initiative? For more information, please visit `https://commongoodcyber.org`.

Cyber Threat Alliance: `https://cyberthreatalliance.org`

Discover the Beyond125 action plan: `https://www.beyond125.org`

Donate time or funds: `https://commongoodcyber.org/donate`

FIRST: `https://www.first.org`

Global Cyber Alliance: `https://globalcyberalliance.org`

Institute for Security and Technology: `https://securityandtechnology.org`

Internet Society: `https://internetsociety.org`

Shadowserver Foundation: `https://shadowserver.org`

PERSPECTIVE: Cyber Civil Society—Common Good Cyber

Civil society uses the Internet in its core missions, from feeding the hungry to improving global health. But civil society faces soaring risks from cyber threats, and it lacks the resources and expertise to respond. This is the most critical cybersecurity challenge for nonprofits. How can they survive and support the common good in a world overwhelmed by online threats?

There are many key approaches, such as increasing volunteerism. Certainly among the most important is increasing the protection of civil society with cybersecurity solutions that work for them and that they can afford—helping ten million nonprofits around the world protect themselves despite their resource constraints. The Common Good Cyber initiative is a collaborative effort, launched by the Global Cyber Alliance and partners, bringing together CSOs, funders, and technical partners to work together to deliver the cybersecurity capabilities that civil society so urgently requires. Its work includes building the effectiveness of those organizations supporting the cybersecurity of civil society, increasing their resources, especially including funding, and raising awareness of the value of their work so that it can be supported by others. These organizations may not be household names, but they enable communities everywhere to thrive. Although their work is vital, their resources are fragile, just like the nonprofits they support. Many operate on razor-thin budgets, relying on tiny donations, grants, and volunteers.

(*continued*)

(*continued*)

Common Good Cyber's plan is both structural and practical. Structurally, we need a cybersecurity-focused nonprofit ecosystem with sustained and consistent investment, shared intelligence, and trusted coordination mechanisms that persist beyond any single crisis or grant cycle. Practically, we need affordable, accessible protection against common threats: safer email and domain infrastructure, scam and fraud defenses, incident readiness, and basic cyber hygiene that actually fit civil society's workflows and budgets.

In just two years, Common Good Cyber has built a community to advance this work, mapped the contributions of nonprofits, built collaboration among nonprofits providing cybersecurity tools and services, and launched the Common Good Cyber Fund. The Fund is designed to support cybersecurity infrastructure and services that protect everyone from digital harm.

The Fund's vision includes investing in shared infrastructure, supporting regional and thematic communities of practice, and enabling early intervention before threats cascade across networks. The Fund also aligns funders around a common framework, so cybersecurity becomes a standard, supported component of civil society work rather than an afterthought.

The Common Good Cyber Fund involves coordinated efforts from the initiative's founders: the Cyber Threat Alliance, Protect·ngo, FIRST, the Global Cyber Alliance, the Global Forum on Cyber Expertise, the Institute for Security and Technology, and The Shadowserver Foundation. The Internet Society is the Fund manager and is itself a large contributor. GCA leads the Fund's Strategic Advisory Committee, composed of experts from around the world.

As digital threats continue to grow in speed and sophistication, civil society cannot afford fragmented, ad hoc defenses. We require collective action—donors, volunteers, industry, and policymakers all playing a role. Together, we can sustain the nonprofits that protect the digital foundation of modern life.

—Philip Reitinger, Chair, Common Good Cyber Fund Strategic Advisory Committee; Senior Advisor and President Emeritus, Global Cyber Alliance

The Global Cyber Alliance works in favor of an Internet fostering human connection, progress, and trust. It puts in place a hands-on approach to making this vision a reality. It offers practical tools that can be used by anyone who is a target in cyberspace in order to ensure their safety.

PERSPECTIVE: Cyber Civil Society—The Internet Society

For the Common Good: Why Civil Society Needs a Digital Shield

Civil society clings to a dangerous myth: that good "cyber hygiene" will protect individuals from even the world's most powerful attackers. Human rights defenders, journalists, and NGOs are urged to use longer passwords, enable two-factor authentication, and keep their software up to date. Make no mistake, these steps are crucial. But against million-dollar spyware attacks, "hygiene" is an unlikely savior.

Too often, civil society is the first target of sophisticated state-sponsored and criminal attacks. Tactics tested on NGOs and journalists today, whether by nation-states or

(*continued*)

(continued)

organized cybercrime, are often unleashed on governments and infrastructure tomorrow. The imbalance is stark: unlimited adversarial budgets versus finite nonprofit resources.

This is a market failure, plain and simple. The companies entrusted with "securing the Internet" mostly secure it for those who can afford it—not out of malice, but because market incentives reward enterprise customers. To make the Internet safe for everyone, we can't keep placing the burden of defense on vulnerable or lower-resourced communities. We need a cyber civil defense: a layered ecosystem that protects the common good by default.

The first layer is the terrain itself. Security cannot be a luxury add-on that users must spend time and money to configure. We must fund and maintain critical cybersecurity infrastructure so that safety is woven into the Internet's very fabric. That means supporting open-source protocols and nonprofit infrastructure providers—the unsung heroes who help keep the Internet safe. This goes beyond encryption; it means, for example, funding the rewrite of the Internet's core code into memory-safe languages to eliminate entire classes of vulnerabilities, and supporting the large-scale sinkholing of botnets before they ever reach a user's device.

When encryption keeps our data private, and when the software we download is hardened to ensure it has never been tampered with, the burden of defense shifts from the vulnerable journalist in a conflict zone onto the infrastructure. It shifts because security is baked into the tools they rely on, effectively removing the "user error" variable entirely.

Even with the safest, most robust terrain, something always gets through. When that happens, there needs to be a safety net. Currently, support is fragmented and ad hoc: if an NGO is targeted, they may know a friendly researcher or a tech company employee who might be able to help—but personal connections aren't a sustainable strategy.

We need a scalable layer of digital first responders. It's time to weave the isolated strands of our current ecosystem—helplines, threat intelligence providers, incident response teams—into a cohesive network. This requires funding the "connective tissue" of the ecosystem—the shared standards and trusted channels that allow defenders to share data instantly rather than comparing notes months later.

When a humanitarian group is targeted, that intelligence shouldn't die in a silo; it should be analyzed and shared to protect everyone. However, sharing requires breaking the silence. The NGO community is often still too inclined to treat cyber incidents as taboo, fearing reputational damage. We must create space for nonprofits to safely discuss threats, transforming individual incidents into public lessons that harden the entire landscape.

When attackers know that targeting one organization will immediately harden defenses across many, the economics of attack begin to shift.

Let's not forget: no defense force survives without supply lines. The biggest weakness in civil society's cyber defense isn't technical—it's economic. The open-source maintainers, the helpline operators, and the policy advocates who defend the Internet are burning out because

(*continued*)

(*continued*)
funding is precarious. Round-the-clock, relentless threats cannot be fought with overly restrictive project grants that force defenders to scramble for survival rather than focus on the adversary at the gates.

To achieve resilience, we must shift from a short-term mindset to a sustainability mindset—offering long-term, unrestricted support that keeps top talent on the frontlines. The "market failure" in cyber defense won't fix itself. That's why we created the Common Good Cyber Fund: to pool resources and build the architecture that brings these layers together—infrastructure, scalable support, and advocacy to protect the vulnerable.

The result is an integrated, resilient shield for civil society. When we treat cyber defense as a public good—not a luxury item—we can build an Internet where journalists, activists, humanitarians, and civil society aren't left to fend for themselves, but are instead protected by the ecosystem we've built together.

—Joseph Lorenzo Hall, PhD; Distinguished Technologist, the Internet Society

The Internet Society is a nonprofit working toward a safe Internet for all. It helps preserve the foundations on which it was originally built and fights for global and safe access, so that it can reach its full potential as a democratic and inclusive space.

Identify: Assessing Risks, Vulnerabilities, and the Threat Landscape

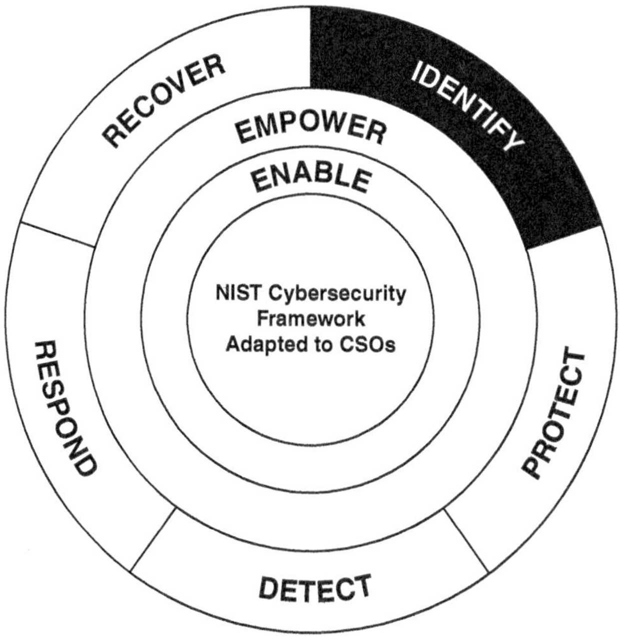

The Identify function lays the groundwork for all cybersecurity efforts by helping CSOs understand what they have, what matters most, and where they are vulnerable. It brings clarity to assets, data, and risks that are often poorly mapped in nonprofit environments. By establishing this foundation, organizations can make informed decisions about where to focus their limited resources. The following solutions show the diversity of possibilities offered to CSOs, from individual organizations to strategic missions from cities, as well as initiatives brought forth by large public institutions.

Hack4Values

What Is It and How Does It Work? Hack4Values is a non-profit initiative that mobilizes ethical hackers to help CSOs identify and fix vulnerabilities before malicious actors can exploit them. Built on the principles of responsible disclosure and community-driven security, the program connects CSOs with vetted volunteer security researchers who perform real-world testing of their digital infrastructure.

The process begins when a CSO joins the program and submits its digital assets for review. Hack4Values coordinates a structured ethical-hacking workflow: reconnaissance, vulnerability discovery, validation, and reporting. Findings are shared privately with the CSO, along with clear remediation guidance. The program emphasizes actionable results rather than theoretical risks, ensuring that even organizations with limited technical capacity can understand and address the issues uncovered.

Hack4Values also works to normalize ethical hacking as a public-interest activity. It advocates for safe legal environments for researchers, promotes responsible-disclosure norms, and collaborates with donors and institutions to integrate preventive cybersecurity into humanitarian and development programs. By bridging CSOs and the global ethical-hacking community, Hack4Values provides a scalable, cost-free model of proactive defense.

Who Benefits from It? CSOs of all sizes benefit directly from Hack4Values' support. Many CSOs lack the resources to commission penetration tests or hire cybersecurity staff, leaving them exposed to preventable vulnerabilities. Through Hack4Values, they gain access to high-level expertise that would otherwise be financially out of reach.

Beneficiaries include humanitarian organizations, human rights defenders, youth and education nonprofits, and grassroots associations. Ethical hacking helps them secure sensitive data, protect field operations, and maintain the trust of donors and beneficiaries. The program also strengthens the broader ecosystem: by reducing the number of exploitable vulnerabilities across civil society, it limits the opportunities for attackers to cause widespread harm.

Ethical hackers also benefit. They gain experience, contribute to meaningful missions, and join a community of practitioners committed to defending the public good. For many, Hack4Values offers a rare opportunity to apply offensive security skills in a context where the impact is immediate and deeply human.

Learn More About Hack4Values

Interested in this initiative? For more information, please visit `https://hack4values.eu`.

Become a volunteer ethical hacker: `https://hack4values.eu/hack-for-a-cause`

Support NGOs: `https://hack4values.eu/ngos-and-nonprofits`

CyberSecure The Hague: NGO Support Program

CyberSecure The Hague is a consortium of nonprofits including Protect[ngo], The Hague Humanity Hub, the Dutch Institute for Vulnerability Disclosure, and CSIRT.global. Partially funded by the City of The Hague, it offers free cybersecurity support to local nonprofits.

CyberSecure The Hague offers cybersecurity assessments, tools, and free training, as well as best practices and tips tailored to the needs of each member organization. Its goal is to strengthen the entire nonprofit ecosystem in The Hague so that organizations can bring the best support possible to communities all around the world.

The positive impacts of this initiative have reached over 135 countries, thanks to the 26 member organizations committed to reinforcing their digital resilience. In total, that amounts to almost 65 million beneficiaries worldwide, whose data is efficiently protected and whose access to help is stabilized.

Learn More About CyberSecure The Hague

Interested in this initiative? For more information, please visit `https://www.humanityhub.org/project/cyber-secure-the-hague`.

The Hague Humanity Hub: `https://humanityhub.org`

Dutch Institute for Vulnerability Disclosure: `https://www.divd.nl`

CSIRT.global: `https://csirt.global`

UnderServed

The main component of UnderServed, an EU-funded project under the Internal Security Fund (ISF), is a platform that serves to report digital threats. It's built on a system that automatically analyzes results and produces reports that are then sent throughout the community as well as to law enforcement. UnderServed is meant to act as a bridge between CSOs and the public sector.

One of the main achievements of the project is the publication of a report titled *Cyber Threat Landscape of EU NGOs*, in October 2024. Its conclusions described a saturated and complex threat landscape and a great vulnerability on the side of CSOs within the European Union. It introduces the platform as the first step in a long-term effort to protect civil society online (Figure 4.5).

Thanks to UnderServed, connections appeared between civil society and law enforcement. By having access to the reports generated by the system, the latter gained deeper knowledge of existing threats and of the ways in which they could support CSOs. They also benefited from employee training focusing on interpreting and exploiting cyber threat intelligence.

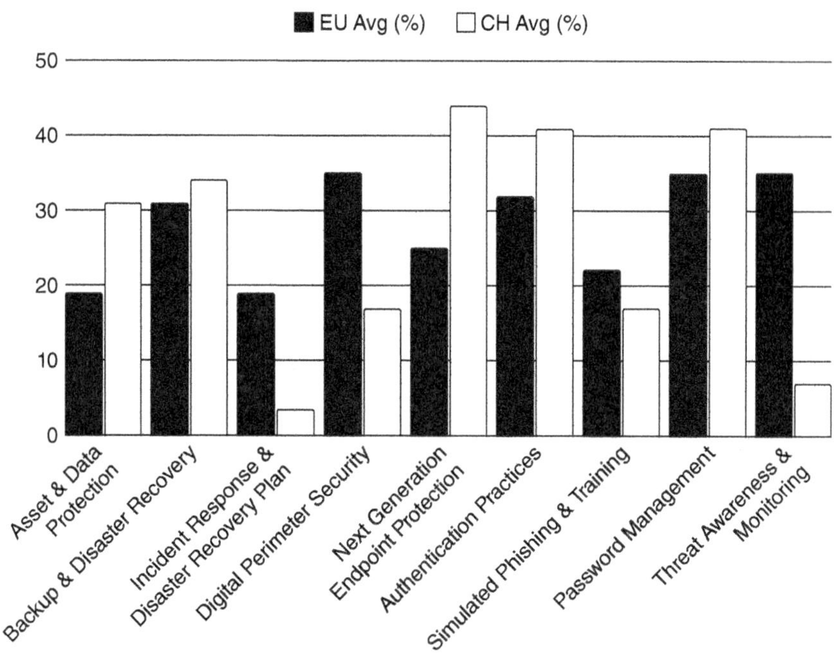

FIGURE 4.5 Average cybersecurity maturity scores of humanitarian NGOs in the EU and in Switzerland.

Source: UnderServed, 2023–2025

Learn More About the UnderServed Project

Interested in this initiative? For more information, please visit `https://underserved-project.eu`.

Read the *Cyber Threat Landscape of EU NGOs* report: `https://underserved-project.eu/deliverables`

PERSPECTIVE: Cyber Civil Society—Hack4Values

Protecting Those Who Protect: Ethical Hacking as a Practical and Sustainable Solution for Civil Society

Humanitarian and civil society organizations operate where vulnerability is highest: conflict zones, disaster areas, fragile political contexts, and communities with limited access to basic services. Yet today, these organizations are increasingly exposed to an invisible but growing threat: cyberattacks.

From my experience working alongside NGOs and cybersecurity practitioners, one reality is undeniable: cyber incidents no longer stop at digital damage. A ransomware attack can freeze an emergency response. A data breach can expose vulnerable populations or put field staff at risk. A service outage can interrupt fundraising at a critical moment and permanently erode donor trust. In several cases, cyber incidents have directly delayed or compromised humanitarian operations on the ground.

The paradox is striking. NGOs are mission-driven, trusted, and impact-focused—yet many lack the resources, internal expertise, or institutional support to manage cyber risk. This makes them disproportionately attractive targets for attackers. Addressing this imbalance is no longer optional; it is a humanitarian necessity.

This is where ethical hacking proves to be a particularly effective, pragmatic, and concrete solution.

Unlike heavy, compliance-driven security approaches that are often costly and slow to deploy, ethical hacking focuses on real-world vulnerabilities identified in real conditions by skilled security researchers acting responsibly. Through mechanisms such as responsible disclosure and bug bounty programs, ethical hackers help organizations detect and fix weaknesses before they are exploited. For NGOs, this means immediate risk reduction and measurable impact, without complex transformation programs or unrealistic investments.

Ethical hacking is effective because it is grounded in reality. It is pragmatic because it prioritizes what truly matters: exploitable vulnerabilities. And it is concrete because it delivers actionable results—clear reports, reproducible findings, and practical remediation paths. Most importantly, it creates durable resilience by embedding a proactive security mindset within organizations.

On the ground, the benefits are tangible. Critical systems are secured. NGO teams gain confidence and visibility over their digital exposure. Beneficiaries—often already in precarious situations—are protected from secondary harm caused by digital failures. Cybersecurity becomes an enabler of humanitarian action, not a burden.

Yet this operational success highlights a broader policy challenge. In many countries, ethical hackers still operate in legal gray zones. Reporting vulnerabilities, even in good faith, can carry legal or reputational risks. This discourages disclosure and weakens collective security. At the same time, cybersecurity is rarely integrated into humanitarian policies or funding frameworks as a core requirement.

(*continued*)

(continued)

Governments and institutions have a crucial role to play by formally recognizing ethical hacking as a public-interest activity, providing legal protections, and embedding cybersecurity into humanitarian support mechanisms. Donors also hold significant leverage: by funding preventive cybersecurity initiatives and encouraging ethical-hacking programs, they protect not only NGOs, but also the impact of every project they support.

This conviction is precisely why Hack4Values was created.

Hack4Values was founded to protect those who protect. Our mission is simple but ambitious: to provide NGOs with free, ethical-hacking-based cybersecurity support, leveraging a global community of volunteer ethical hackers. We believe that cybersecurity should not be a privilege reserved for large corporations, but a common good accessible to organizations serving the public interest.

This approach has already demonstrated its impact at scale. Today, more than 20 NGOs in France and Europe—ranging from small grassroots organizations to large international actors—are actively protected through ethical-hacking initiatives. These include organizations such as Action Against Hunger, Handicap International, UNICEF, Médecins Sans Frontières, SOS Méditerranée, Apprentis d'Auteuil, e-enfance, Terre des Hommes. . .

In 2025 alone, over 500 real and exploitable vulnerabilities were identified across their digital systems. Each of these findings was documented, prioritized, and followed by direct support to help NGOs implement rapid and effective remediation. These are not theoretical risks, but concrete weaknesses whose correction has immediately strengthened operational resilience.

By connecting NGOs, ethical hackers, donors, and institutions, Hack4Values demonstrates that a collaborative, offensive-yet-ethical approach to cybersecurity is not only possible, but essential. In an increasingly digital world, cooperation is our strongest defense—and ethical hacking is one of its most powerful tools.

—Fabien Lemarchand, President, Hack4Values

Protect: Data, Technology, and Talent

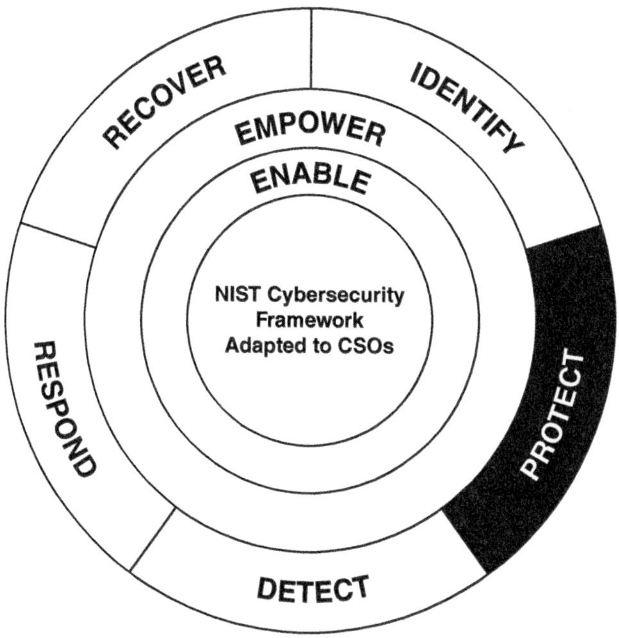

The Protect function focuses on the safeguards that keep CSO systems, data, and people secure. It covers practical measures like access control, training, and secure configuration—areas where nonprofits often face constraints due to mixed technology setups and limited staff capacity. Strengthening this layer helps reduce the likelihood and impact of attacks. Here again, various possibilities arise, from hands-on tools to large-scale initiatives aiming to bring change on a systemic level.

GCA Cybersecurity Toolkits

What Are They and How Do They Work? The Global Cyber Alliance is part of the network of CSOs whose purpose is to protect humanitarian actors and essential service providers in cyberspace. As part of its mission, it has put together cybersecurity toolkits adapted to various publics and situations, which can ensure a certain level of digital hygiene in a simple way.

The different toolkits contain guides full of hands-on information to assess users' initial cybersecurity level and strengthen it through simple measures. They grant access to efficient software: password manager, authentication software, antivirus, VPN, automatic-update software. . . By acquiring a toolkit, users can also access informational resources, a blog, and a forum.

Who Benefits from Them? The Global Cyber Alliance offers five different toolkits:

- **Individuals**: For individuals who wish to strengthen the safety of their devices and personal data
- **Mission-based**: For CSOs
- **Journalists**: For journalists, with a particular focus on the free press
- **Small businesses**: For small to medium businesses
- **Elections**: For election officials, with the aim of protecting a free and fair democratic process

GCA cybersecurity toolkits are meant to be used by many actors in society and to have a positive impact in terms of human rights, freedom, and democracy. Their adaptability makes them an essential asset for those who feel endangered by cyber threats.

Learn More About the GCA Toolkits

Find out about the various available toolkits: `https://gcatoolkit.org`

Protect your nonprofit: `https://gcatoolkit.org/mission-based-orgs`

Suggest a tool: `https://gcatoolkit.org/application-for-inclusion-in-the-gca-cybersecurity-toolkit`

Support the Global Cyber Alliance: `https://globalcyberalliance.org/donate`

OSPREY

OSPREY (Online Safety and Security for Protection of Public-Facing Professionals and Democratic Resilience) is an EU-funded project dedicated to protecting professionals who have acquired a certain level of visibility or notoriety. It leverages AI, awareness efforts, and targeted campaigns to ensure the safety of journalists, politicians, and others who strive to defend human rights.

OSPREY provides access to a knowledge pool regarding threats faced online by public-facing professionals (PFPs) and the best ways to protect them. The initiative also seeks to understand which actors pose the greatest risks, their motives for attacking, and the most effective defense mechanisms.

Practically speaking, OSPREY shares its conclusions with PFPs and the organizations they work for through toolkits and training sessions. It also serves to inform and train political leaders in the hopes of encouraging them to put in place relevant measures. Lastly, it aims to educate the public on the dangers encountered in cyberspace, in particular by PFPs, and on the means available to protect against them.

Learn More About the OSPREY Project

Interested in this initiative? For more information, please visit `https://cordis.europa.eu/project/id/101225639`.

Cybersecurity Clinics

What Are They and How Do They Work? Cybersecurity clinics are structures that are put in place in universities, offering cybersecurity support for organizations, but also for local and regional public institutions and small businesses. They rely on the work of students and are similar to cyber-volunteering programs, with the distinctive feature of being linked to the place of education of their volunteers, who are not (yet) private-sector employees. Volunteers are generally studying computer science, but can also be enrolled in programs focusing on journalism, political science, law, business. . .

Today, this practice is mostly present in the United States; this is where you can find the Consortium of Cybersecurity Clinics, put in place by UC Berkeley, which is also home to the first cybersecurity clinic, opened in 2018. The objective of the Consortium is to increase the number of clinics in the country while paying special attention to the involvement of female and minority students, who are largely underrepresented in the cybersecurity field.

Who Benefits from Them?

Supported Organisms Cybersecurity clinics offer a different kind of solution to CSOs who are vulnerable in cyberspace and seeking to strengthen their resilience despite a limited budget. At this point, you know all about the benefits of this free support.

The clinics do not focus exclusively on civil society and extend their services to other types of beneficiaries. These are generally small structures that play an essential role within the local community. When they thrive in a safe and long-lasting way, the entire population wins.

Student Volunteers We've also discussed the benefits reaped by volunteers in similar programs (see the Builders and Cyber Resilience Corps). The case of cybersecurity clinics is unique in this sense as well, as the volunteers happen to be students at the university that the clinic is affiliated with. They gain a valuable experience: the opportunity to apply their skills, sometimes for the very first time, to situations outside an academic context. It's a first step beyond the theoretical framework of university and a chance to generate real impact with their work.

> **Learn More About Cybersecurity Clinics**
>
> US Consortium of Cybersecurity Clinics: `https://cybersecurityclinics.org`
>
> Cyren ZH (Zurich, Switzerland): `https://cyrenzh.ch/cybersecurity-clinic`
>
> Glasgow Caledonian University Cybersecurity Clinic (Glasgow, UK): `https://gcu.ac.uk/aboutgcu/academicschools/sse/cybersecurityclinic`

PERSPECTIVE: Donors and Foundations—Google.org

Talent, Training, and Technology: A Blueprint for Civil Society Resilience

CSOs make up the foundations of our societies and democracies. They enable access to skills and resources, provide essential aid, protect human rights, and hold power to account. Yet, in the digital domain, nonprofits, along with other critical community infrastructure organizations such as hospitals and schools, reveal the sector's soft underbelly: they often hold the most sensitive data, but possess the fewest resources to protect it. It's a vulnerability that we cannot afford to ignore.

We cannot, however, rely solely on market solutions to close this gap. We need a paradigm shift from cybersecurity as a luxury for the well-resourced to cyber resilience as a public good, embedded in every organization. At Google.org, we believe that to protect vulnerable organizations at scale, we must align our efforts across three pillars: talent, training, and technology.

- Talent: Building a human firewall

  Ultimately, resilience is about people. The global shortage of cyber talent—estimated by ISC2 to be around 4.8 million practitioners globally—is our most significant collective vulnerability. And we don't just need more professionals; we need experts from diverse backgrounds who understand local contexts. That's why we launched Google.org's Cybersecurity Clinics and Seminars program, modeled after medical teaching hospitals, to train university students on cyber skills and serve as a vital pipeline, bringing women and nontraditional students into the field. By funding these educational pathways, we are not just filling jobs; we are building a diverse "human firewall" that reflects the societies it protects.

- Training: Connecting skilled resources with community needs

  CSOs lack the in-house expertise and often can't afford to employ the experts needed to identify their cyber weaknesses and build their defenses. A critical part of the Cybersecurity Clinics (US and APAC) and Cybersecurity Seminars (EMEA) programs is teaching students to provide pro bono digital defenses to under-resourced organizations under the guidance of faculty. Currently running at over 60 universities globally, the model is on track to provide expert-level protection to 7,000 organizations by 2030. We have also piloted pathways to scale in APAC to meet regional demand by equipping a network of local partners with skills and resources to cascade the learning to their respective communities. This train-the-trainer model decentralizes expertise and has enabled 180,000 organizations so far to access foundational cyber training.

- Technology: Democratizing defense

  Attackers are increasingly using enterprise-grade and AI tools to target civil society; nonprofit defenders need to narrow the gap in terms of cyber defense capabilities. In Europe, for example, over half of nonprofits lack structured incident tracking, and Protect$^{.ngo}$'s research shows that only 10% have a formal response

(*continued*)

(continued)

> plan in place. That's why the European Democracy Resilience Network, led by Protect·ngo, aims to provide NGOs with a "digital shield"—leveraging AI to analyze threat data and share real-time intelligence. In addition, at `Google.org`, we're looking at how to secure the foundational layers of these organizations—from hardening websites and databases to automating identity management. This moves the sector from reactive to proactive, tech-enabled defense.

True resilience can't be bought, and it isn't going to be a quick fix. We need to build it not in silos, but through sustained collaboration and co-funding, fostering partnerships across governments, philanthropy, and industry to back these scalable models together.

—Rowan Barnett, Director, `Google.org` EMEA, APAC

Google's philanthropy applies Google's innovation, research, and resources to promote progress and expand opportunity for everyone, focusing on the fields of Knowledge, Skills and Learning; Scientific Progress; and building Stronger Communities. It supports nonprofits, civil entities, and academic institutions with funding, products, and technical expertise, and has supported 3,600 institutions in over 160 countries.

PERSPECTIVE: Cyber Civil Society—Project Galileo

At Cloudflare, we have always believed the Internet should be an open space that fosters the exchange of knowledge and ideas. This commitment dates back to our earliest days, when we began providing free cybersecurity services to ensure that security is accessible to everyone on the Web, regardless of their financial resources or technical expertise. Our goal is to make it easier for people to access secure tools to build and launch ideas anywhere in the world.

With a global network spanning 330 cities in over 125 countries, Cloudflare has the infrastructure and engineering resources to help NGOs stay secure. That's why we launched Project Galileo in 2014, to protect vulnerable, public-interest websites—specifically independent journalists and human rights defenders—from the massive, targeted DDoS attacks designed to silence them. Today, the project has grown to cover more than 3,000 entities across 120 countries, and mitigates approximately 9.9 billion attacks targeting vulnerable groups every month. To achieve this, we partner with 58 CSOs to help us identify which areas of the world could benefit from our help, and what kind of tools best support civil society's evolving cybersecurity needs. Project Galileo protects groups working on a range of causes, including digital rights, voting and election integrity, healthcare, the environment, art, and more, ensuring that those working on the frontlines of the world's most pressing issues remain secure and reliable.

Over the last decade of Project Galileo, Cloudflare has continuously expanded its suite of tools to keep pace with increasingly sophisticated attacks against vulnerable groups. This support includes securing public-facing websites to ensure they remain fast and reliable during increases in traffic or targeted cyberattacks. For internal security tools, Zero

(*continued*)

(*continued*)

Trust services act as a digital shield, protecting staff from phishing, malware, and accidental data leaks while ensuring sensitive information is accessible only to authorized users. As part of helping NGOs prepare for an AI-driven future, Cloudflare provides tools to secure AI applications, mitigate complex threats like prompt injections, and help organizations safely adopt evolving digital technologies. By providing these resources, Cloudflare aims to give NGOs peace of mind that their data is secure and their voices will remain online, allowing them to stay focused on their essential work and growing impact.

We view Project Galileo as a core way to fulfill our mission to democratize access to secure tools, ensuring that the defenders of democracy have the same technical protections as the world's largest businesses. Ultimately, Project Galileo is built on the belief that every voice on the Internet deserves protection. Our partnerships do more than defend websites; they preserve an inclusive digital landscape where knowledge thrives and the tools of empowerment remain accessible to all.

—Jocelyn Woolbright, Program Manager, Cloudflare Impact Team

Detect: Monitoring and Intelligence

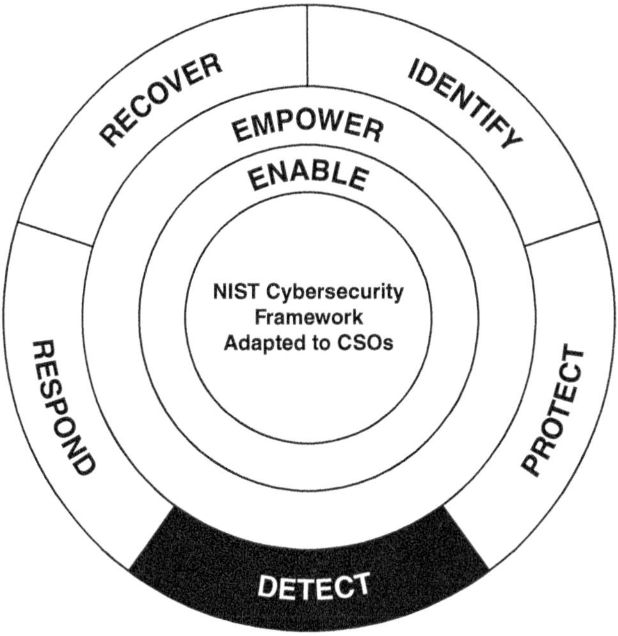

The Detect function ensures CSOs can spot suspicious activity or emerging threats before they escalate. For organizations working in sensitive contexts, early warning is essential to prevent data leaks, targeted attacks, or operational disruption. Building detection capabilities gives CSOs the visibility they need to act quickly and confidently. Let's dive into the solutions that exist to catch threats as early as possible and avoid destructive attacks.

The Shadowserver Foundation

What Is It and How Does It Work? The Shadowserver Foundation is one of the world's largest nonprofit cybersecurity organizations, dedicated to improving Internet safety through large-scale threat monitoring and free daily reporting. Shadowserver operates a global sensor network that continuously scans the Internet to identify compromised systems, exposed services, malware infections, and other indicators of risk.

Organizations can register their networks to receive daily remediation reports. These reports highlight vulnerabilities, misconfigurations, and signs of compromise, along with guidance on how to address them. Shadowserver also collaborates with law enforcement agencies and major infrastructure providers to dismantle botnets, take down malicious servers, and coordinate global cyber defense operations.

For CSOs, Shadowserver's services act as an early-warning system. Many nonprofits lack the tools or staff to monitor their networks continuously. Shadowserver fills this gap by providing high-quality, actionable threat intelligence at no cost, helping organizations reduce exposure before attackers exploit it.

Who Benefits from It? Any organization with an Internet presence can benefit from Shadowserver's free reporting, but the impact is especially significant for under-resourced groups such as CSOs, independent media, and community organizations. These groups often operate with minimal cybersecurity budgets and limited visibility into their digital risks.

By receiving daily alerts, CSOs can detect compromised accounts, outdated systems, or exposed services early—before they escalate into major incidents. Shadowserver's global perspective also helps nonprofits understand how broader threat trends may affect their sector.

Governments and infrastructure operators benefit as well. Shadowserver's data supports coordinated takedowns, national cyber defense strategies, and public-interest research. Its work strengthens the entire Internet ecosystem by reducing the number of vulnerable systems available to attackers.

Learn More About The Shadowserver Foundation

Interested in this initiative? For more information, please visit `https://www.shadowserver.org`.

Register for free daily reports: `https://www.shadowserver.org/what-we-do/network-reporting/get-reports`

Become a partner: `https://www.shadowserver.org/partner`

European Democracy Resilience Network

The European Democracy Resilience Network (EDRN) is an EU-funded initiative coordinated by Protect.ngo and EU DisinfoLab. Its objective is to create a blueprint to protect democratic spheres, particularly when it comes to information manipulation.

When the EDRN was launched in September 2025, the 30 member CSOs took a survey that revealed alarming results. Seventy-nine percent had been targeted by information manipulation before; 52% had been the victims of organized campaigns; and only 10% had come up with a detailed incident response plan. Three common challenges were identified: the frequency with which CSOs were exposed to information-manipulation campaigns, their inability to efficiently monitor threats, and their lack of technical means and organizational solutions.

Now that these issues have been identified, the EDRN's goal is to create a blueprint that can be applied to all member CSOs and beyond in order to ensure their protection in cyberspace. This blueprint would include a monitoring aspect to detect any potential threat, a precise incident response plan, as well as tools, training, and support to ensure long-term resilience.

Learn More About the EDRN Project

Interested in this initiative? For more information, please visit `https://edrn.protect.ngo`.

Read the *Kick-Off Workshop Summary Report*: `https://protect.ngo/resources/research/edrn-kick-off-workshop-summary-report`

Read the *EDRN Blueprint Report*: `https://protect.ngo/resources/edrn-blueprint-report`

EU DisinfoLab: `https://www.disinfo.eu`

PERSPECTIVE: Cyber Civil Society—The Shadowserver Foundation

In the current cyber landscape, resilience and business continuity are no longer boardroom buzzwords. In practice, they translate into one question: how do we prevent cyber incidents from becoming major liabilities and operational crises? Cyberattacks are fast, indiscriminate, and can lead to operational, financial, and reputational harm for an organization. Most incidents start in very ordinary ways: a convincing message, a rushed click, a reused password, a setting accidentally left open, or a patch in an externally exposed service not applied. Organizations are targeted for a variety of reasons: their financial situation, their size, the nature of their work, or simply because the attackers identified an easy path into their network. The bottom line: every organization is at risk of a cyberattack.

For NGOs, independent journalists, and community critical groups, the impact of a cyberattack can be greater, as they often have less dedicated staff and fewer resources to aid in response and recovery. The challenge can be greater when the situation involves political pressure or intimidation.

Attackers seek efficiency. Every organization must ask: what is publicly exposed, who has access, and how quickly can exposure be reduced to mitigate threats? Consideration must include websites, edge devices, remote-access portals, cloud storage links, and shared admin accounts, among others. It also requires understanding which accounts have high privileges, which suppliers connect into your systems, and what data is reachable if a credential is stolen. Having this knowledge allows organizations to close attack paths before, rather than after, damage occurs.

A baseline exists—though it is not easy to maintain in practice:

- Protect accounts: Set strong authentication checks (like two-step verification) and avoid reuse of passwords.
- Reduce what's exposed: Remove or secure edge devices and old accounts, and keep devices and apps updated. Patch!
- Make email harder to fake: Reduce impersonation and "fake sender" scams that trick staff and donors.
- Be on the lookout for things out of place: Have a simple plan for "what to do if something feels wrong."
- Be ready to recover: Keep backups and practice restoring access, so the organization can keep operating.

An organization cannot effectively prioritize its cybersecurity efforts without current, verifiable, high-quality cyber threat intelligence (CTI). CTI provides decision support, identifying what is vulnerable and exploited, and how a sector is being targeted. While access to actionable CTI can reduce exposure at scale, commercial CTI can be quite costly and often not directly relevant, posing a significant problem for NGOs with limited budgets and resources for interpretation.

(*continued*)

(*continued*)

This is where free, community cybersecurity resources, including those provided by The Shadowserver Foundation, can be especially helpful. Shadowserver's free daily CTI, in the form of network remediation reports, alerts organizations to potential pre-breach and post-breach situations to help facilitate remediation. Think of it as an early-warning and guidance service that is constantly watching the Internet and providing free, regular reports that can help under-resourced organizations identify risky exposures or signs of compromise early, so they can be fixed before escalating to a critical breach.

Shared community knowledge, discipline, and continuous improvement are critical to reducing risk, mitigating harm, and improving resilience. NGOs and other under-resourced groups should be strongly encouraged to collaborate with cybersecurity nonprofits, including Shadowserver and Protect.ngo, that can provide free tools and services to help improve cybersecurity hygiene and better secure their networks.

—The Shadowserver Foundation

PERSPECTIVE: Cyber Civil Society—The Cyber Threat Alliance

In the modern era, every organization faces cyber threats. However, CSOs are exposed to a wider, more complex range of threats than many other organizations due to their involvement in political, governmental, and humanitarian issues. Alongside the common cybercriminal activities plaguing purely commercial entities, civil society is also targeted by nation-states and hacktivists. Further, the threats to civil society often extend beyond the digital realm into the physical world, affecting civil society personnel in multifaceted ways and compounding their problems. The complexity of the threat environment for most civil society organizations is hard to overstate.

At the same time, CSOs typically struggle to resource their cybersecurity needs. They often have minimal budgets but operate large, distributed networks serving vulnerable populations. Their security needs are broad, covering infrastructure, data, staff, donors, and constituents, but most security providers generally do not offer such a broad spectrum of services at prices civil society can afford. The mismatch between threat and available resources contributes to civil society being attractive targets to threat actors, including nation-states and hacktivists.

How should CSOs manage in such a high-threat/low-resource environment? While no organization can reduce its cyber risk to zero, CSOs can substantially reduce their risk without spending huge amounts of money, deploying lots of complex technology, or impeding workflow. Implementing a few practices can change an organization's risk profile, even against sophisticated actors. Further, these steps are not all or nothing; partial implementation will still improve an organization's cybersecurity. These practices include:

Changing the mental frame—In a digital world, cybersecurity is not a technical luxury but a critical mission enabler to ensure that clients, customers, and recipients receive appropriate services; donors have confidence that

(*continued*)

(*continued*)

resources will reach intended recipients; and staff are digitally protected. Further, successful cybersecurity does not mean keeping all bad actors out of all networks and devices all the time; instead, success means that bad actors cannot use cyber tools to disrupt an organization's operations over the long term, or to harm its personnel.

Leveraging free and accessible resources—Over the past few years, an array of nonprofit organizations has emerged that focuses on civil society cybersecurity, including NetHope, Protect·ngo, and the Non-Governmental Organization Information Sharing and Analysis Center (NGO-ISAC). They provide numerous tools and resources, such as phishing training, tabletop exercises (TTXs), and comprehensive guides.

Implementing five basic controls—Despite the bewildering array of solutions available, five actions can dramatically reduce an organization's risk: using a password manager or shifting to passkeys; using multi-factor authentication whenever possible; updating software regularly; filtering links in emails; and backing up data regularly. A handy mnemonic for these actions is PAULB (Password Manager, Authentication, Updates, Links, Back up).

Digital threats to civil society are not going away anytime soon. The good news, though, is that defending against them is not impossible. With the right mindset, resources, and controls, civil society organizations can dramatically reduce their risk and increase their resilience.

—Michael Daniel, President and CEO of the Cyber Threat Alliance

The Cyber Threat Alliance is a nonprofit acting as a bridge between different organizations and companies in the cybersecurity ecosystem in order to share intelligence. Its sharing platform allows members to report threats and exchange information to strengthen their resilience.

Respond and Recover: Collaboration, Follow-Up, and Rehabilitation

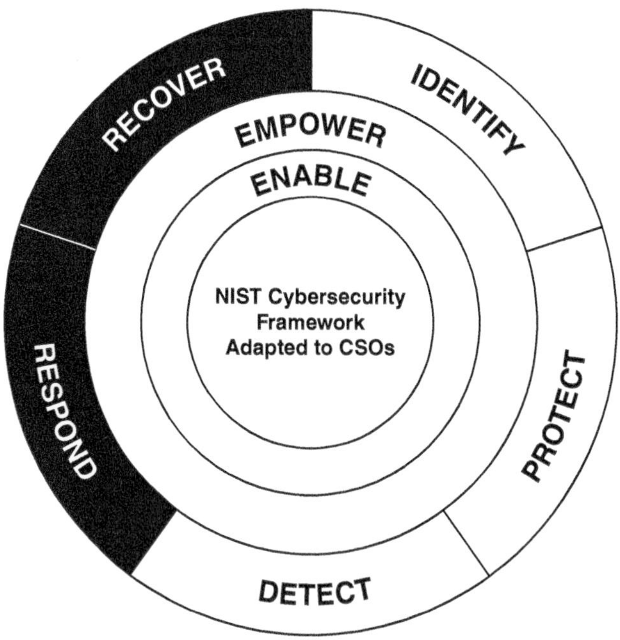

The Respond and Recover functions focus on helping CSOs contain incidents quickly and restore stability afterward. They ensure that, once a threat is detected, organizations can act to limit damage, coordinate effectively, and return to normal operations with minimal disruption to the communities they protect. By emphasizing structured processes, shared knowledge, and continuous improvement, these functions strengthen a CSO's ability to withstand crises should they happen and emerge more resilient each time. Many solution models exist to bring support to CSOs following an attack: if you are looking for help after an incident, you will most likely find your match in the following list.

NGO Information Sharing and Analysis Center (NGO-ISAC)

What Is It and How Does It Work? The NGO Information Sharing and Analysis Center (NGO-ISAC) is a CSO that offers a civil society community portal in which all members are seeking to strengthen the cybersecurity of their organizations. It currently hosts hundreds of professionals working for US-based nonprofits, who help each other daily by exchanging tips and best practices. Each week, they receive information from industry experts who aim to keep them updated on threats existing in cyberspace.

For CSOs who wish to go further, NGO-ISAC offers free additional services: a tailored coaching program; a mentorship program to facilitate knowledge sharing; and an annual conference where members can meet their peers and dig deeper into certain topics.

Who Benefits from It? Any NGO based in the United States can become a member of NGO-ISAC. Participants gain access to a community of nonprofit professionals working toward a common goal and showing solidarity by exchanging information regularly about the latest threats and best practices to adopt in order to avoid harm. Beyond practical tips, the sense of community brought to nonprofit members through these kinds of spaces reminds them that they are not alone, that others face similar challenges, and that initiatives are being developed specifically to bring them the help they need.

NGO-ISAC also gives cybersecurity experts the chance to join its Partner Program. By doing this, professionals can leverage their skills to help important causes, train themselves on how their work can apply to civil society specifically, and share knowledge with those who need it.

Learn More About the NGO Information Sharing and Analysis Center

Interested in this initiative? For more information, please visit `https://ngoisac.org`.

Join the community: `https://ngoisac.memberclicks.net/member-application#!`

NetHope

What Is It and How Does It Work? NetHope is a global consortium of leading humanitarian and development nonprofits working together to strengthen digital resilience across the sector. By pooling expertise, negotiating collective technology solutions, and sharing threat intelligence, NetHope helps its members address cybersecurity challenges that no organization can tackle alone.

NetHope operates the Global Humanitarian ISAC, a trusted space where CSOs exchange real-time information about cyber threats, vulnerabilities, and incidents. Members receive contextualized alerts, technical guidance, and coordinated support during crises. NetHope also provides training, tabletop exercises, and capacity-building programs to help organizations improve their cybersecurity maturity.

A key part of NetHope's model is collaboration with private-sector partners. Technology companies contribute tools, expertise, and resources tailored to the needs of humanitarian organizations. This partnership model ensures that nonprofits gain access to enterprise-grade protection adapted to their operational realities.

Who Benefits from It? NetHope has over 60 member organizations, including some of the world's largest humanitarian actors, but the benefits extend far beyond them. By strengthening the cybersecurity of major CSOs, NetHope indirectly protects millions of beneficiaries whose data and safety depend on secure digital systems.

Smaller organizations also benefit through shared resources, open guidance, and collective threat intelligence. NetHope's work reduces the risk of cascading breaches across the humanitarian ecosystem, where interconnected operations mean that a compromise in one organization can affect many others.

Private-sector partners benefit as well: they gain insight into the unique challenges faced by nonprofits and contribute to solutions that have global humanitarian impact.

Learn More About NetHope

Interested in this initiative? For more information, please visit `https://nethope.org`.

Explore NetHope resources: `https://nethope.org/resources`

Join the community: `https://www.tfaforms.com/5195751`

Forum of Incident Response and Security Teams (FIRST)

What Is It and How Does It Work? FIRST is a global association of incident response and security teams dedicated to improving the effectiveness of cybersecurity response worldwide. It brings together security professionals from governments, companies, universities, and nonprofits to collaborate on best practices, coordinated response, and trusted information sharing.

Members of FIRST gain access to a global network of experts who support each other during incidents, share technical insights, and develop standards that guide the cybersecurity community. FIRST also organizes training programs, conferences, and working groups that help organizations build and maintain robust incident response capabilities.

For nonprofits, FIRST provides a bridge into the broader cybersecurity ecosystem. Many CSOs lack formal incident response teams or established relationships with national CERTs (Computer Emergency Response Teams). By joining FIRST or partnering with FIRST-affiliated teams, they gain access to expertise, frameworks, and trusted channels that are essential during crises.

Who Benefits from It? Organizations that participate in FIRST benefit from a global community of responders who can provide guidance, support, and intelligence during incidents. This is particularly valuable for CSOs, which often face sophisticated threats but lack the resources to respond alone.

FIRST's work also benefits the broader Internet ecosystem. By promoting coordinated vulnerability disclosure, standardized response practices, and cross-border collaboration, FIRST helps reduce the impact of cyberattacks worldwide. Its members play a critical role in mitigating large-scale incidents, supporting takedowns, and improving global cyber resilience.

Nonprofits, in particular, gain access to a level of expertise that would otherwise be inaccessible. Through FIRST, they can connect with trusted responders, receive early warnings, and adopt proven response strategies.

Learn More About FIRST

Interested in this initiative? For more information, please visit `https://www.first.org`.

Explore membership: `https://www.first.org/membership`

Learn about incident response standards: `https://www.first.org/standards`

Attend FIRST events: `https://www.first.org/events`

Nonprofit Cyber

What Is It and How Does It Work? Nonprofit Cyber is a coalition of cybersecurity CSOs. It is composed of over 50 member organizations and aims to create connections within the ecosystem in order to foster unity, collaboration, and communication. It also works to make these CSOs and the topics they address more visible.

Thanks to the exchanges brought by Nonprofit Cyber, cybersecurity CSOs can align to offer the most efficient support and advice possible to their beneficiaries. The results obtained through collaborative projects are publicly available (Figure 4.6). On its website, you can find common guidance on passwords as well as an index of existing solutions, with a search tool based on your needs and criteria.

FIGURE 4.6 The Nonprofit Cyber search tool.
Source: Nonprofit Cyber, 2026

Who Benefits from it? As we've established, collaboration and mutual support within the cybersecurity CSO ecosystem benefit not only the organizations, but also the millions of beneficiaries they protect worldwide. The goal is to build collective resilience and reduce cybercrime as a whole, particularly when it targets vulnerable communities.

Thanks to the tools available on its website, Nonprofit Cyber can benefit any individual, organization, or company that wishes to be informed and apply stricter norms to protect itself online.

Learn More About Nonprofit Cyber

Interested in this initiative? For more information, please visit `https://nonprofitcyber.org`.

Common Guidance on Passwords: `https://nonprofitcyber.org/common-guidance-on-passwords`

Nonprofit Cyber Solutions Index: `https://nonprofitcyber.org/nonprofit-cyber-solutions-index`

PERSPECTIVE: Cyber Civil Society—FIRST

Preparing Civil Society for Cyber Threats: Why No Organization Can Face This Alone

Civil society organizations occupy a unique and dangerous position in the cyber threat landscape. They hold sensitive data about vulnerable populations, activists, and humanitarian operations, yet often operate with IT budgets that are a fraction of corporate security spending. Attackers know this. Whether they are state-sponsored groups targeting human rights defenders or ransomware gangs seeking victims, NGOs are increasingly targeted.

The uncomfortable truth is that most organizations only discover their security gaps mid-crisis. When systems fail and donor data is compromised, teams realize they lack tested playbooks, clear escalation paths, or trusted contacts who can help. By then, it's too late. A minor incident can become an existential threat.

This is why preparation matters more than any single security tool you could buy. The organizations that recover fastest from cyberattacks, whether government agencies, corporations, or humanitarian groups, aren't necessarily the ones with the biggest budgets. They're the ones embedded in incident response (IR) communities before crisis hits.

These networks provide what no platform can replicate: direct access to subject matter experts worldwide who, in many cases, have already handled your exact scenario; shared intelligence on emerging threats; and localized guidance from professionals who understand your region's specific challenges. For example, when a ransomware variant spreads or a vulnerability threatens your infrastructure, members of trusted IR communities learn about it in hours through peer channels, not weeks later through vendor alerts.

But community access isn't enough. You also need strong foundational security practices. Network segmentation keeps attackers from moving freely between systems if they breach your perimeter. Multi-factor authentication stops compromised passwords from becoming open doors. Retiring old credentials and decommissioning legacy access prevents yesterday's employee accounts from becoming today's backdoor. These aren't glamorous solutions, but they stop more attacks than any expensive platform ever will.

Equally critical is treating cybersecurity as a mission-critical function, not simply an IT problem. When a breach affects donor trust, program delivery, or beneficiary safety, it becomes a leadership issue affecting the entire organization. Regular exercises involving senior staff help validate response capabilities and improve decision-making before real pressure hits. Having a response plan, even an imperfect one, transforms potential crises into manageable situations.

Here's what most organizations miss: you cannot solve this in isolation. No single NGO has the resources, intelligence, or expertise to defend against nation-state actors or sophisticated criminal groups without support. The organizations that survive and recover are those already connected to trusted IR communities.

Joining networks like the Forum of Incident Response and Security Teams (FIRST) or regional CERTs gives you access to real-time threat intelligence, peer assistance, and proven response frameworks developed by teams who've faced these attacks before. Further, law enforcement cooperation, coordinated disclosure, and shared defense strategies all depend on trust built over time, not scrambled phone calls during an emergency. The IR community operates on a simple principle: we're stronger together than any of us are alone.

—Chris Gibson, CEO, FIRST

PERSPECTIVE: Cyber Civil Society—NetHope

Why Community Is the Only Viable Cybersecurity Strategy for Nonprofits

It is well documented that nonprofits face state-level cyber threats with start-up-level resources. But the deeper story is structural. Nonprofits share implementing partners, second staff to each other, loan laptops in the field, use common platforms, and co-deliver programs funded by the same donors. Staff paid by different agencies sit at the same desk. Data and devices move across organizational boundaries in ways unthinkable in the corporate world.

This is a constantly shifting supply chain where personal relationships and shared values are the primary currency, invisibly prompting people to compromise organizational boundaries "for the mission." Trust is passed from hand to hand, much like a trust token in a credit-card transaction. These networks are anything but linear and are incredibly suited to the fluidity of humanitarian crises. Yet the philosophies used to secure businesses do not survive in these contexts. A breach at any point compromises everyone downstream and laterally. No single organization can secure itself in a system this porous on its own.

Consider the May 2021 Nobelium/USAID hack. Russian state-linked actors impersonated USAID's email platform and hit 3,000+ accounts across 150+ organizations. The phishing worked because these organizations routinely open emails from their biggest funder. The attack weaponized the network of trust itself. Many subsequent breach stories show a pattern of secondary and tertiary breaches that ripple outward, far beyond the targeted agencies.

The sector's vulnerability is not a failure of awareness but a consequence of its interconnected nature. Technical training alone hits a plateau. We need cybersecurity at the community layer, so it becomes part of the work itself. In a credit-card transaction, tokens pass from merchant, through processor, to clearing bank, each link at a different compliance level, yet all invested in the transaction's integrity. Beneficiary data travels the same way: from local partners, through field laptops, to a coordinating INGO, to a donor's system, where it is exposed at every handoff. No single merchant secures the whole payment chain alone; the industry created PCI-DSS standards and shared fraud networks because risk is distributed. Similarly, when your nonprofit partner's unsecured laptop is your data breach, individual resilience is an illusion.

The NetHope Global Humanitarian ISAC is the practical embodiment of shared-chain defense and resilience. Launched in 2022 by NetHope, USAID, Okta, and Protect.ngo, it is a global, sector-wide ISAC for humanitarian nonprofits. It builds the shared layer through contextual threat intelligence, staff skilling, unified standards (so the trust token travels a common baseline), and collectively negotiated technology. Like clearing infrastructure, it does not replace each organization's security but creates the shared intelligence layer that makes individual defenses meaningful.

Every hand that touches the token bears responsibility. *Donors* must fund cybersecurity as core infrastructure and fund collectives like ISACs that lift the whole network. *Nonprofit leaders* must join threat-sharing communities and break the silence around breaches. *Technology partners* must embed protection by design in nonprofit licenses. *Policymakers* must extend humanitarian law into cyberspace.

(*continued*)

(*continued*)

In a world of digital identities and digital targeting, a data breach can be as deadly as a misdirected airstrike. The nonprofit sector's greatest asset has always been its willingness to work across boundaries with high trust. Now, the ethic of mutual aid must extend to mutual defense. Community is not just the best cybersecurity strategy; it is the only one.

—Dianna Langley, COO and Interim CEO, NetHope

PERSPECTIVE: Cyber Civil Society—NGO-ISAC

In the past 25 to 30 years, the way we work has changed significantly. We use the Internet to exchange information, money, and everything else. That open exchange makes our society much more efficient, but also much more vulnerable to cybercrime—and because civil society is underfunded and understaffed, it does suffer more than large companies. In that sense, the work we are doing is vital and increasingly interconnected—and most importantly, though we haven't been fully successful, I wouldn't say that we are failing either.

Problems and Solutions

Many of the problems we face require a combination of different solutions. Imagine a three-legged stool. The first leg is organizations like ours that provide cybersecurity and technology capacity at low or no cost to civil society. The second leg is vendor partners who provide solutions to civil society actors. The third leg is foundations and funding mechanisms that have the ability to support solutions. In the middle of those three legs, if they are effective, is a low-risk, high-trust organization or set of organizations. One area in which we haven't been very effective as a group is acting in unison so that we can achieve this goal together. We need to think about how these three legs can work in conjunction.

Another problem with cybersecurity, from the point of view of nonprofits, is that they see the cost, but not the reward—the attacks that are prevented from happening. The return on investment is hard to measure. Sometimes negative reinforcement may work: if an organization experiences an incident, it may be willing to go through the effort of implementing more controls, because it has seen the cost of attacks occurring. Positive reinforcement is harder: there is no incentive to invest in cybersecurity. This may be a place where funders, the third leg of the stool, can have an impact—financial incentives may encourage non-profits to use more cybersecurity tools.

The Role of NGO-ISAC

Our organization is meant to be a lighthouse. We want high-risk CSOs, and generally anyone who wants to increase their cybersecurity, to be able to work together through our community. Each person has a particular set of skills that could be useful to someone else.

We are also a place for private-sector partners to help civil society. This can be done directly—someone asks a question and a private partner jumps in to offer help. It can also simply be a way to reach the community in an easy,

(*continued*)

(*continued*)
casual format—for example, to let them know about civil-society-specific opportunities that they may offer, such as grants or donations.

Going Forward

We need to get rid of the shame associated with cybercrime. Victims often feel they are at fault because they didn't have a strong password or were using the wrong software. But take these situations and move them into the real world: if someone breaks into your CFO's office and steals the file in her desk, she wouldn't be blamed for not having a better lock on her door. The fault would fall on the criminal for breaking in.

Eradicating the shame that surrounds cyberattacks would encourage victims to tell their story and help others avoid similar attacks. It would also shift the onus onto the people committing the crime, because they are the ones who should feel ashamed.

—Ian Gottesman, founder and CEO, NGO-ISAC

Sources

Duguin, Stéphane and Marta Rodilla Álvarez. "The Threat Landscape Facing Civil Society." *Philea*, December 4, 2025, `https://philea.eu/opinions/the-threat-landscape-facing-civil-society`

International Civil Society Centre and Protect·ngo. *Navigating Cybersecurity: Guidance for (I)CSO Professionals*. April 2022. `https://icscentre.org/wp-content/uploads/2025/09/Cybersecurity-guidance.pdf.pdf`

International Civil Society Centre and Protect-ngo. *Open Letter to Governments, Corporations and Philanthropies* (Civil society CEO call). August 26, 2024. https://protect.ngo/nonprofits-call

World Economic Forum. *The Global Risks Report 2026*. January 2026. https://reports.weforum.org/docs/WEF_Global_Risks_Report_2026.pdf

Methodology

Scope

The research and analysis presented in this book focus on attacks against civil society organizations, nonprofit organizations, nongovernmental organizations, charities, and associations around the world. (As explained in Chapter 1, these terms are used interchangeably throughout.) Generally speaking, the book does not seek to draw comparisons against the context of other sectors. Inasmuch as their respective impact and arguable severity may vary, the book outlines the predominant threats that have affected civil society as a whole.

Consultations have taken place with cybersecurity professionals, chief information security officers (CISOs), CSO staff, donors, volunteers, and victims of attacks on CSOs as part of the drafting and review process to encourage transparency and ensure that claims are corroborated by those working directly with or in civil society.

Sources

For the cases of cyberattacks or information manipulation discussed in this book, as well as the tools and solutions presented, the primary research method was desk-based and conducted in English, French, and Spanish. The main categories of data sources were:

- Primary data through direct engagement with CSOs. This data was collected via surveys, interviews, focus groups, and testimonials drawn from Protect·ngo's work with nonprofits.
- Secondary sources including (but not limited to):
  - Statements and articles by CSOs and other civil society actors
  - Cybersecurity firm reports and threat intelligence databases
  - Official governmental and law enforcement publications
  - Academic studies
  - News media and other publicly available open-source repositories

Privacy and Data Consideration

To protect the privacy and safety of the organizations and individuals mentioned, this book deliberately omits specific details regarding their identities or vulnerabilities.

The cybersecurity insights presented in this book are derived from external cybersecurity intelligence platforms and publicly available information. No intrusive scanning, penetration testing, or direct access to any organization's internal systems was conducted. Instead, the examples are based on observations of cybersecurity posture, threat intelligence, and exposure data that provide insights into sector-wide risks.

This book does not assess individual organizations but rather provides sector-wide insights into systemic cybersecurity risks. The conclusions are based on publicly observable indicators and aggregated risk data, ensuring that no sensitive details about any specific organization are disclosed. By identifying common security challenges, the book aims to inform proactive resilience strategies that benefit the entire sector.

Glossary

Accountability The degree to which a threat actor or stakeholder can be held accountable for actions, or failures to act, that may contribute to increasing threats.

Attribution The process of identifying and tracking down which threat actor is responsible for an attack. Attribution may take place at a technical, political, or legal level.

Business Email Compromise A type of cyberattack in which criminals imitate company/organization email addresses and impersonate leaders or trusted staff members in order to deceive employees into making or approving wire transfers.

CEO Fraud An operation in which the leader or a high-ranking employee is impersonated in order to deceive staff members for financial gain. This can be done via email (see Business Email Compromise), text message, phone call, or even video call.

Civil Society Organization (CSO) A vast range of associations, NGOs, nonprofits, and other groups with a social purpose, working for the common good and social progress. They may define themselves using various terms depending on their structure, financing, or legal status. These organizations are committed to the public good, responding to humanitarian crises, granting access to drinking water, fighting hunger, providing healthcare, combating violence against women, and opposing child labor, sexual exploitation, and human trafficking.

Cyberattack An attack conducted by a threat actor using a computer network or system with the intention of disrupting, disabling, destroying, controlling, manipulating, or surveilling a computing environment, infrastructure, and/or data.

Cybercriminal A person who commits crimes using a computer network or system (cyberattacks).

Cybersecurity The application of technologies, processes, and controls to protect computer systems, networks, and data from unauthorized disclosure, theft, or damage. The goal is also to reduce the risk of cyberattacks.

Cyberspace Digital systems and the online world make up cyberspace, which covers everything accessible through computer networks and the Internet. This includes everything from corporate networks and social media platforms to bank accounts and cloud services. It also includes all connected appliances, such as video surveillance cameras, gaming consoles, TV sets, or robot vacuum cleaners.

Cyber Volunteering Volunteering in the field of computer science and cybersecurity. In our particular case (Cyber Builders, see Chapter 4), volunteers are private-sector employees donating their free time and leveraging their skills to help CSOs.

Dark Web An overlay network within the Internet that can only be accessed with specific software, configurations, or authorization (e.g., TOR, Freenet, I2P, or ZeroNet) intended to defend digital rights by providing security, anonymity, and censorship resistance. Though it is used for legitimate reasons, it has been heavily used by criminals, and the term "dark web" nowadays is generally associated with websites (also called onion sites) that are specifically used for criminal purposes.

Data Breach The exposure of confidential, sensitive, or protected information to an unauthorized person. This could be accidental, such as a USB drive left on a train or an email attachment sent to the wrong person, but it can also be deliberate, as when malicious actors access a network and exfiltrate (target, copy, and transfer) data.

Deepfake An AI-generated or AI-manipulated image, audio, or video file impersonating an individual.

Disinformation The sharing of intentionally false or misleading information. (See Information Manipulation.)

Distributed Denial-of-Service (DDoS) DDoS is an attack technique used to flood a network, service, or server with excessive traffic to cause it to cease functioning normally. It is said to be distributed when the source of the attack is composed of a multitude of devices or systems.

Doxxing The disclosure, often on the Internet, of private information about an organization or individual without their consent.

Hacktivist An individual acting alone or in a group, leading cyberattacks for ideological motives.

Information Manipulation A behavioral pattern that threatens or can potentially have negative impacts on political values and procedures. It is defined by a conscious and coordinated attempt at manipulation. (See Disinformation.)

Internet A series of technologies that allow computers and networks to communicate with each other.

Malware Malicious software. These are pieces of code designed to damage, destroy, or subvert computer systems. This includes viruses that can replicate and stop systems from working; ransomware, which blocks systems until a ransom is paid; and spyware, which is hidden on the target system and spies on the device users.

Multi-Factor Authentication Authentication using more than one factor. This includes passwords or PINs, cryptographic authentication devices, facial or digital recognition (biometric).

Phishing An operation through which criminals access a device's system and data. It is often a way to get hold of elements that are not sufficiently protected, subsequently allowing for cyberattacks.

Ransomware A type of malware conceived to extort money by encrypting or blocking access to files or to a computer system until a ransom is paid.

Snackable Content A type of content that is short, appealing, and made for quick consumption. It is mainly visual and is often found on and associated with social media.

Spyware A type of malware conceived for espionage and surveillance. It discreetly gathers data from one device and transfers it to another.

Social Engineering The psychological manipulation of a person in order to induce them to divulge information or complete an action.

Stakeholder Any person, group, sector, or entity in a position to play an active role in changing the attack threat landscape.

State Actor A threat actor directly or indirectly colluding with a nation-state (e.g., state actor or state-sponsored actor).

Threat Actor A person or entity acting in cyberspace with the intention of harming other people, entities, or computer systems.

Victim A person who is impacted, either directly or indirectly, following a cyberattack (e.g., a CSO worker, collaborator, or beneficiary).

World Wide Web The WWW is a system of websites and web resources accessed through browsers using the HTTP/HTTPS protocols.

Acknowledgments

I extend my deepest gratitude to all the people who supported us during the writing process and contributed to this book through their experience and expertise:

Amira Dhalla (Aspen Digital), Andrew McCracken (Protect·ngo Executive Board and WaterAid International), Ann Cleaveland (UC Berkeley Center for Long-Term Cybersecurity), Chris Gibson (FIRST), Dianna Langley (NetHope), Fabien Lemarchand (Hack4Values), Gabriel Anthony Lopre (Fondation suisse de déminage), Ian Gottesman (NGO-ISAC), Jeroen van den Berg (City of The Hague), Jocelyn Woolbright (Project Galileo), Joseph Lorenzo Hall (Internet Society), Justin Spelhaug (Microsoft Elevate), Michael Daniel (Cyber Threat Alliance), Nicolas Haddad, Nuno Abano (European Climate Foundation), Philip Reitinger (Common Good Cyber), Richard Andrew (Peace Direct), Rowan Barnett (Google.org), The Shadowserver Foundation, Thomas Rubatscher (SOS Children's Villages), Wolfgang Jamann (International Civil Society Centre), as well as Laetitia Pulido for the work she provided in the context of her studies at the University of Lausanne.

I would also like to thank our Executive and Advisory Board members for their continuous support of our activities, and the companies and foundations that contributed to creating Protect·ngo: Mastercard Center for Inclusive Growth, Microsoft, the Ford

Foundation, and the William and Flora Hewlett Foundation. Our work would be nonexistent without your support.

A huge thanks from the bottom of my heart to all current and former Protect·ngo staff. This book is a testimony to their efforts and dedication to protect civil society every day. You'll read from some of them in this book, Adrien Ogée, Alexandru Lazar, Fabien Leimgruber, Florent Bitschy, Inês Narciso—but it takes many hands on deck to keep our work going.

Among this group, warm thanks to Laure Salathé and Marta Rodilla Álvarez—without whom this book would never have seen the light of day—and Bruno Halopeau—without whom I would never have had the opportunity to write it.

Finally, a special thanks to Elena Gkiola, who saw the need for this book before anyone else.

All proceeds generated from the sales will be invested in the digital resilience of civil society, in particular via the Cyber Builders and Tracer programs.

About the Author

In today's world, conflict doesn't begin on the battlefield—it starts in cyberspace.

Stéphane Duguin, born in Saint-Étienne (France), has spent his career tracking those who weaponize technology against the most vulnerable. As CEO of Protect.ngo, he leads efforts to defend the defenders—civil society professionals targeted by cyberattacks and information manipulation.

Formerly at Europol, he led major international operations against cybercrime, terrorism, and hybrid threats.

With publications in international fora and high-level briefings to the European Parliament and the United Nations Security Council, he brings a rare, insider perspective on the invisible conflicts shaping global security today.

Index